How to Think Like a ... *Behavior Analyst*

Understanding the Science That Can Change Your Life

by Jon S. Bailey and Mary R. Burch

 Routledge
Taylor & Francis Group
New York London

Routledge
Taylor & Francis Group
711 Third Avenue
New York, NY 10017

Published in Great Britain by
Routledge
Taylor & Francis Group
2 Park Square
Milton Park, Abingdon
Oxon OX14 4RN

International Standard Book Number-13: 978-0-8058-5888-4 (Softcover)

Library of Congress Cataloging-in-Publication Data

Catalog record is available from the Library of Congress

Visit the Taylor & Francis Web site at
http://www.taylorandfrancis.com

and the Routledge Web site at
http://www.routledge.com

Dedication

To my mother, Noreen Bailey, who never understood what I did,
and to Jack Michael, who understood everything.
—*Jon Bailey*

And to my husband, who said, "You ought to write books."
—*Mary Burch*

Contents

Preface

Behavior analysis has often been described as "the best kept secret in psychology." As a well established, evidence-based treatment approach based on learning theory, behavior analysis has been making a significant difference in the lives of many thousands of developmentally disabled individuals for 40 years. Behavior analysis procedures have been developed to teach basic self-help skills, functional language, and community access repertoires to individuals with disabilities and to allow them to live and enjoy rich and varied lives.

The very same procedures have been used in special education classrooms and standard elementary school settings, where teachers are now able to take control of their rowdy, out-of-control students and produce model students who complete their homework on time, are respectful of others, and who enjoy learning.

Still other applications of behavioral procedures include training parents and foster parents to use the power of positive reinforcement to lovingly raise children who listen, take responsibility, and actively participate in family life. This field, applied behavior analysis, caught fire in 1993 with the publication of the best-selling, true-life story of Catherine Maurice and her two autistic children. Frustrated by pediatricians, psychologists, and psychiatrists—who essentially told her that her autistic child would need to be institutionalized—Maurice sought help on her own and discovered the groundbreaking work of Ivar Lovaas. Lovaas showed with intensive behavioral treatment, up to 50% of autistic children could recover. Ms. Maurice found a behavior analyst therapist, and as we say, the rest is history. *Let Me Hear Your Voice: A Family's Triumph Over Autism* (Maurice, 1993)was an overnight sensation with parents all over the United States. Suddenly, the best kept secret was out in the open, and a huge demand for qualified behavior analysts was created. Within 10 years, over 50 graduate programs emerged that were approved to teach behavior analysis and a certification program, the Behavior Analyst Certification Board®, began testing and certifying behavior analysts to meet the sudden need. Now undergraduate students all over the country are taking courses on operant conditioning, learning theory, functional analysis, behavioral theory, research methods, and ethics, and graduate students are learning the professional skills necessary to bring this technology to families, schools, rehabilitation settings, and more. With this boom in popularity, there seemed to be a need for a book that would help the beginning student (as well as consumers and the everyday citizen) understand what this fascinating field was all about.

This is a book for everyone who is concerned with behavior. *How to Think Like a Behavior Analyst* answers questions that are often posed by college students, parents, employers, employees, and professionals who work with humans or animals. Ideas, trends, techniques, and practical information pertaining to the exciting field of behavior analysis are presented in a concise, user-friendly format.

The question-and-answer format of *How to Think Like a Behavior Analyst* answers 50 frequently asked questions about behavior analysis. Each of the informative answers is presented in an educational and entertaining manner.

Using this book as a guide, beginners in psychology and behavior analysis can learn about how behavior analysts work, why specific methods and procedures are used, and what it takes for treatment to be considered effective.

For parents and teachers, *How to Think Like a Behavior Analyst* provides basic background information and detailed examples of how behavior analysis can be used to help children. Employers and employees will learn how behavior analysis is used in work settings in the questions pertaining to performance management. Everyone can learn how to make life better by being able to use positive reinforcement with people and situations encountered every day.

Specific topics covered by *How to Think Like a Behavior Analyst* include basic questions such as how behavior analysis is different from psychotherapy, what analysis involves, and the meaning of evidence-based treatment. The section on Applications gives tips on using behavioral procedures to improve lives and deal with others, as well as illustrating in some detail how behavioral procedures are used in community settings. In the Science and Technology section, we answer questions about the science behind behavior analysis and discuss the issue of finding "causes " of human and animal behaviors. In General Issues, we answer important questions about behavior analysis in groups and discuss the significance of the concept of history of reinforcement. Behavior analysts have a unique take on other fields and here we describe our views of counseling, the medical or disease model of behavior, and discuss the important issues of motivation and emotions. As most scientists are, behavior analysts are skeptical of unverified methods, and in Basic Skepticism we take on several popular but unproven methods, such as facilitated communication and sensory integration. There are a certain number of myths about the behavioral approach covered in Myths and the Media. In this section, the reader gets our take on Dr. Phil and the Supernanny as representatives of behavior analysis in the media. Or not. To round out the book, we have an extensive section written specifically for students on Getting Started in a Career in Behavior Analysis; finally, we discuss the Code of Ethics for this new breed of professionals.

As you read *How to Think Like a Behavior Analyst,* you will realize the widespread applications of behavior analysis as a field and just how important it is for everyone to understand how behavior works.

How to Think Like a Behavior Analyst is not a theoretical or academic work. Our goal was to write an informative book that is practical, simple, clear, direct, and fun to read. But don't let the user-friendly nature fool you; underneath it all is the message that being trained in behavior analysis can improve your life and the lives of those around you.

—JSB
—MRB

READER NOTE

Throughout the text we use the term *behavior analyst* as a generic term to describe various professional titles such as *applied behavior analyst*. The original founders of the applied side of the field got their laboratory training in operant conditioning from researchers in the experimental analysis of behavior and early on referred to themselves as *behavior modifiers* or *behavioral engineers*. Only recently (mid-1990s) has a true profession emerged and given us the official designation of *Board Certified Behavior Analyst*™. While we use this term occasionally throughout the book, somehow the simple term *behavior analyst* seems sufficient to convey the meaning we are trying to convey. Further, practitioners also use the terms Certified Behavior Analyst (CBA) and Board Certified Behavior Analyst (BCBA) interchangeably. The terms Certified Associate Behavior Analyst and Board Certified Associate Behavior Analyst are also used interchangeably by practitioners.

In addition, we should acknowledge that this work is the result of the authors' combined 50-plus years of experience in the field; we do not claim that it represents the views and opinions of all behavior analysts.

ACKNOWLEDGMENTS

We gratefully acknowledge the assistance of Dawn Bailey (no relation) in reviewing an early draft of this manuscript and in getting feedback from the students in her applied behavior analysis class during the summer of 2005.

We would also like to thank Jeanine Plowman Stratton and Matt Normand, who provided thoughtful and extremely helpful suggestions in their detailed reviews of the manuscript, which ultimately made this book better.

Another person who played an invaluable role in this process was the amazing Mandy Newham, our illustrator. Mandy listened and heard what we were asking for in all of the illustrations and, coming to the project late in the process, she broke the land-speed record in getting the drawings done before deadline.

And finally, we need to thank our friend, guru, and marketing mentor, Al Cuneo, for convincing us that a great book deserves a great cover.

Introduction

I am fascinated by human behavior, and I have been for over 40 years. While I'm shopping at the local mall or waiting to catch my next flight in a bustling, crowded airport, I thoroughly enjoy people watching. A few years ago, I almost missed a plane because I was so enthralled by a frustrated mother who was traveling with her two small children. One child was happy to sit quietly and read a book, whereas the other was climbing all over mom, loudly demanding attention, and driving her and everyone in the waiting area absolutely crazy. What had me spellbound was the manner in which this well intended mother was using her attention both wisely and unwittingly at the same time. Missy, who could have been cast in any movie role requiring a perfect little girl, was about 5 years old. She sat to her mom's right, reading quietly to herself from a children's book. When she would occasionally come upon a word she didn't know, she'd look up at her mother and carefully spell the word. "E-L-E-P-H-A-N-T," Missy would read, and mom would supply the individual phonetic sounds, "ELL-EE-F-NT." This literary duo had clearly had done this before, and mom had probably taught Missy to read in just this way, giving her a book at her level or slightly above, then reinforcing this sweet, precious, intelligent child for asking politely for assistance. Precocious little Missy was poised and confident, the picture of the perfect student-to-be.

Enter Jack, Missy's little brother. Jack, on the other hand, was getting reinforced for exactly the wrong behaviors. The unfortunate downward spiral of Jack's behavior began when he was awakened abruptly from a nap. A clumsy, oblivious businessman walked by in a hurry and bumped Jack with his briefcase. Whimpering, Jack climbed up in his mother's lap and laid his face on her chest. She caressed him and tried to get him to go back to sleep, but no such luck. The CNN Airport Channel was loud and exploding with breaking news, the airport was hot and stuffy, and Jack became restless. He reached out with his stubby little finger and gently touched mom on the nose. Mom laughed as she turned to Missy to provide assistance with another difficult word. Jack repeated the touching, but mom was distracted, so he gave her nose a little poke. She jerked her head back, cut him a look, and then laughed again. Over the next few minutes I saw behavior shaping going on before my very eyes. Missy was being rewarded for quiet reading and Jack was being consistently reinforced for the ever more forceful poking that soon evolved into punching mom in the chest.

This young mother had no idea the very same principles she used quite successfully for years with Missy were about to be her undoing with soon-to-be-labeled "bad boy" Jack. I heard the ticket agent shout, "Final boarding call," and I had to get on the plane. Looking back over my shoulder while I was in line, I observed Jack's escalating problem behaviors, "No, no, Jack, don't hit Mommy in the face [giggle, giggle], or Mommy will have to spank you." "Giggle, giggle" was the reinforcer that was about to lead to a major scene right there in the departure lounge.

If I had only had a video camera (and permission to film) to capture this classic behavioral episode on tape, I could have used it in my applied behavior analysis class as a perfect example of the right and wrong ways to use reinforcers. As a behavior analyst, I believe I was witness to a pivotal event in the lives of these total strangers, something that would start a chain reaction that could end up with mom seeking professional help for Jack in a year or two. I might be wrong; other contingencies might have come into play for this family, and Jack might have turned out fine. But for most families, my experience has been parents who bring their 5-, 6-, and 7-year-old children in for behavioral treatment began shaping severe inappropriate behaviors over the span of a few years using reinforcement just as it was used with Jack. When these exhausted and embarrassed parents finally arrive to ask for behavioral assistance, many are at a loss to know how this happened.

Sadly, many children frustrate and confound their parents so badly they are ultimately abused. Or worse. And, saddest of all, it is all totally unnecessary. There is absolutely no reason for parents to become frustrated with their children. If parents only knew how to think like behavior analysts, they would see how the environment influences their children's behavior both physically and socially, and they would use careful observation and some trial and error to identify reinforcers for shaping desired behavior. Parents (or significant adults in the household) with the ability to think like behavior analysts would be able to reinforce children for listening attentively, following instructions, and doing daily chores and nightly homework. There would be much less conflict in these homes as the parents, partners, spouses, grandparents, guardians, nannies, and babysitters in the home became more loving and attentive and learned to use reinforcers effectively.

If more people knew the basic principles of behavior, they would lead happier, less stressful lives. Just think, if you could analyze the behavior of people around you and determine some of the reasons for their actions, wouldn't that give you some sense of understanding? If you could use your knowledge to improve your own behavior and subtly influence the behavior of your roommate, partner, spouse, family member, annoying phone-calling relative, or officemate, wouldn't that be a lot better than putting up with (and complaining about to others) irritating, obnoxious, or bossy behaviors? Learning to think like a behavior analyst means having an ability to step back from the human drama playing out before you to find out what is going on so that you can take effective action. Your students aren't following instructions? Maybe the instructions need to be presented in a more effective fashion. Are they sloppy or careless in their work? Maybe you aren't noticing the careful work often enough and handing out praise that means something to these individual learners. These are common problems with easy solutions that can make life better every single day.

Behavior analysts have a worldview of the human condition that is different from almost any other professional perspective. We view human behavior as largely learned and subject to change, if the right variables are put into play.

Amusing behavior, creative behavior, irritating behavior, aggressive behavior; it is all simply learned behavior to us. And if it was learned, we are curious about how that came about. If the behavior is desirable, we would like to reproduce those conditions so that others can benefit. Learning to think like a behavior analyst means becoming a very good observer, and knowing what to look for. We look for consequences in the environment—immediate consequences—and we look for patterns of behavior. Sometimes the consequences are very subtle, a turn of the head or a little smile of recognition. At other times they are obvious, such as when in a meeting one person takes the conversation off track consistently when a certain topic is mentioned. A behavior analyst would immediately see this as an escape/avoidance response, whereas others in the room might prefer to simply pigeonhole him and move on, "That David, he's just a ditz; he can't keep track of anything and I'm getting tired of him." Behavior analysts are always thinking in terms of behavior programs to help solve difficult interpersonal conflicts. My own mantra for dealing with frustrating individuals is, "Shaping, shaping, always shaping."[1]

Behavior analysts also think about measuring behavior and how it can be quantified and analyzed. We're always interested in improving human behaviors, making them more resilient, more robust, more accurate and timely. As a behavior analyst, I think a lot about world peace and the causes of conflict between nations and religions, and special interest groups. I think about how the whole world would be a better place if everyone knew more about how to manage their own behavior and the behavior of others using positive reinforcement and other basic principles. I think about the problems facing the world today and realize that the basis for so many of these problems boils down to the reinforcers of individuals or groups—oil, money, power, or the promise of eternal life.

Behavior analysis is not merely a set of tools to analyze and change behavior, it is a profession with a set of values that we hold dear but rarely

---

[1]Shaping is a procedure for changing behavior that starts with setting the criterion for reinforcement just a little higher than it was previously. When used carefully and precisely over time, it is possible to create entirely new behaviors.

discuss with other people. For example, most behavior analysts like to see people being independent; we would like to see people acquire scores of effective skills so that they don't have to depend on others. We would like to see caring behaviors, and considerate behaviors, and thoughtful, tolerant behaviors. We would like for more people to appreciate the good behavior in the world around them and to reinforce it more often. As behavior analysts, we would encourage respectful behavior and fair, truthful behavior. These are values that are professed by many, but exercised by few.

As behavior analysts, we think constantly about improvement of human behavior in nearly every setting. As I dine out with my wife, I find myself not only appreciating how lucky I am to be married to such a wonderful, talented, beautiful, intelligent woman but also thinking, "That waiter is not attending very closely to my water glass; it's empty, and I've moved it to the edge of the table so he can see it, but he just walks by, oblivious. I wonder what it would take to change his behavior. I wonder how he was trained. I wonder if anyone has ever pointed this out. Most customers won't; they'll just sit and fume." And as I exit the restaurant, I think, "This parking lot could be set up differently. If they had the employees park over there on the last row, there would be more spaces for customers and we wouldn't have to walk so far. They might even get more business ..." "Yes, sweetheart, it is a beautiful night, just look at the stars ..."

And for some reason, my wife says she finds it more relaxing to eat at home.

Isn't *Thinking Like a Behavior Analyst* an oxymoron?

Good point. An oxymoron is when two contradictory or incongruous terms are used together: *jumbo shrimp, plastic glasses,* and *bigger half* are all oxymorons. Some people are under the impression that behavior analysts don't believe in thinking, so a book called *Thinking Like a Behavior Analyst* might seem like an oxymoron.

B.F. Skinner, the godfather of behavior analysis, was a behaviorist through and through. He argued in several of his books thinking is indeed just another behavior people engage in and that thinking could be analyzed just as any other behavior. Skinner argued that as a behavior, thinking had antecedents—some stimuli in the environment that set the occasion for the behavior—and consequences that maintained it. In his book *Verbal Behavior* (Skinner, 1957),[2] Skinner devoted an entire chapter to thinking. As you can tell from the previous paragraphs, behavior analysts think a lot about many different topics. Sometimes this is followed by conversation so that others can find out what we're thinking. Some of the thinking is not worth repeating out loud, so we just edit this and give you the good stuff. So behavior analysts believe in thinking, engage in thinking, and understand thinking is sometimes followed by consequences that maintain it, just like any other behaviors that can be reinforced. Learning to think like a behavior analyst means seeing the world the way we do, and reacting to it the way we do.

We hope you'll enjoy this little book and that you will find it interesting and useful. If you're interested in behavior analysis, you may want to take a course at your local university or read another book on the topic. You'll find a list of books to help you do this in the References section at the end of the book.

—*Jon Bailey*

HOW TO USE THIS BOOK

This book was written to acquaint readers with the field of applied behavior analysis. We believe that parents, teachers, college students, business managers, and anyone else who has an interest in human behavior (either out of curiosity or as part of a job) will benefit from this brief overview of the field.

College instructors will find *How To Think Like a Behavior Analyst* is an excellent choice for a supplemental text for regular general psychology, careers in psychology, behavior modification, or applied behavior analysis courses. The exercises that follow each question can be used to stimulate lively discussions in role-play and other active learning situations.

---

[2]*Verbal Behavior*, published in 1957, is a major treatise that explains in behavioral terms the complex nature of communication among humans.

Parents of autistic children who receive behavioral services will find this book a useful tool for helping to understand some of the basic principles of behavior and for providing insight as to how therapists think about behavior. *How To Think Like A Behavior Analyst* is the book you need when you want to learn about or teach behavior analysis in an educational, jargon-free, and entertaining way.

Chapter

One

Basic
Concepts

QUESTION #1.
What is behavior analysis? Is it psychotherapy?

One of the earliest cases in our field (Wolf, Risley, & Mees, 1964) provides us with an outstanding example of how behavior analysts and clinical psychologists have different perspectives regarding human behavior.

"Dicky" was a 3-year-old child with multiple severe behavior problems. In the early 1960s he was referred to pioneering behavior analysts Mont Wolf, Todd Risley, and Hayden Mees at the University of Washington. As a result of cataract eye surgery when he was a little over 2 years old, Dicky was required to wear special corrective lenses or lose his vision entirely. For more than a year, Dicky's parents struggled with futile attempts to get him to wear the glasses. Dicky not only would not wear his glasses but would throw such severe tantrums he became unmanageable and had to be institutionalized. At the time he was referred to the behavioral team in Washington, Dicky had been diagnosed at different times as mentally retarded, autistic, psychotic, brain damaged, and schizophrenic. These varying diagnoses were the result of multiple behavior problems that included lack of normal social and verbal repertoires, poor eating habits, head banging, face slapping, hair pulling, and face scratching. At the advice of their family physician, Dicky's parents tried restraints, sedatives, and tranquilizers, all to no avail. Finally, Dicky was admitted to a children's mental hospital where more precise treatment could be offered. Enter our groundbreaking behavior analysts; Wolf et al. (1964, p. 311) took one look at the interaction between Dicky and his mother and instantly knew what the problem was: she was reinforcing the behavior (not intentionally, mind you) with her "ineffectual fussing." Dicky's problem was in large part the result of out-of-whack social contingencies, not retardation or supposed childhood schizophrenia. The solution: The behavioral team decided to use *time-out*, which had never before been documented in a case like this. *Time-out* involves separating the child from all sources of reinforcement for a short time, contingent on inappropriate behavior—in this case the severe tantrums. Dicky was returned to the hospital ward environment as soon as the tantrum stopped. Result: within 2½ months, the severe head banging, hair pulling, and face scratching was reduced to zero. Zero.

Although this is only part of the story, it exemplifies many key features of the way that behavior analysts think—and act. First, this was a single case, one child in desperate need of therapy. In addition, Drs. Wolf, Risley, and Mees were interested in taking the case because it represented a complex set of *socially significant behavior* of near life-threatening proportions. They quickly determined that these were *learned behaviors* and they were fairly sure they could identify the *maintaining variable* (the mother's attention) and they knew how to get control by having the child treated in the hospital (where they could train and supervise the staff) rather than at home (where they would not).

After demonstrating clear and dramatic control over this most serious behavior, the behavior analysts then proceeded to attack the remaining problems by *shaping* glasses wearing, treating glasses throwing (which developed soon after), implementing successful interventions for teaching verbal behavior, and finally tackling the messy problems of food throwing, food stealing, and eating with fingers. In each case Wolf et al. (1964) observed the target behavior, looked for controlling variables, and then instituted a change in procedures to reduce and then eliminate the inappropriate behavior (food throwing, food stealing, eating with fingers) or teach new behaviors (eating with a spoon, learning to name pictures, naming objects in his environment, and, later, to answer simple questions such as, "Where are you going tonight?").

> **"We think that it is important to treat *socially significant behaviors,* not just to study them, but to actually analyze and provide treatment, "**

Dicky improved enough within 3 months to make his first foray to his home, where his parents (with the training they had received from the behavior analysts) were able to put him to bed without his having a severe tantrum. In 3 more months, he was gradually faded back into the home and the parents were given full training for all of Dicky's significant behaviors.

This is a perfect example of some fundamental ways that behavior analysts think. We think it is important to treat *socially significant behaviors,* not just to study them, but to actually analyze and provide treatment, *effective treatment*—treatment that works to produce a socially significant change in behavior, not just a tiny statistically significant change but a real-life, dramatic change that everyone can see. To Wolf, Risley, and Mees, Dicky was not a "subject" in an experiment, he was a troubled little boy with a family who loved him and wanted him to be at home and live a normal life. Although unstated, it was clear this was the goal of our pioneering behavior analysts when they took on this original landmark case over 40 years ago. Finally, Wolf et al. (1964) were not satisfied to simply change the behavior; they wanted to *generalize the results* to Dicky's home setting. It was important to this team of behavior analysts that the parents learn how to manage their son's behavior.

This study is a classic in the field, not just because it represents one of the earliest demonstrations of how behavior analysts think and treat behavior, but for the final comment from Dicky's mother after he had been at home for 6 months: "Dicky continues to wear his glasses, does not have tantrums, has no sleeping problems, is becoming increasingly verbal, and is a new source of joy to the members of his family."

Behavior analysis does not resemble any of the traditional forms of psychotherapy and most behavior analysts do not consider themselves psychotherapists.

So, to answer the original question, is this psychotherapy? We would argue that behavior analysis is a form of therapy that falls within the large class of nonmedical treatments for mental and behavioral disorders. As you can see from this example, it does not resemble any of the traditional forms of psychotherapy and most behavior analysts do not consider themselves psychotherapists.

●●●

Key Concepts:
Behavior analysis addresses socially significant behaviors, learned behaviors, maintaining variables, effective treatments, and the generalization of behavior.

EXERCISES:

1. Make note during the next couple of days of the behavior of people around you. Do you see any that present socially significant problems that could benefit from some sort of behavioral intervention?
2. Now, using the Internet go to the Web page for the *Journal of Applied Behavior Analysis* (http//:seab.envmed.rochester.edu/jaba/) and using keywords, see if you can find any articles describing treatments for such a behavior.

QUESTION #2.
It's called *behavior analysis;* just what does *analysis* mean and how exactly do you *analyze* someone's behavior?

The "analysis" part of *behavior analysis* refers to our search for maintaining variables that prompt a behavior and for those that keep it going. We always do this before a treatment is devised; you might think of it as a way of finding the "cause" of a particular behavior. For example, let's say that you observe that a friend-of-a-friend of yours, named Kevin, is constantly interrupting the conversation when you get together for tailgate parties or other weekend social functions. You might talk to your friend about him, "That guy is such a jerk; I don't know why you even hang out with Kevin. I think you should dump him." Or you might say, "He's got self-esteem problems, all he wants to do is talk about himself, did you ever notice how he's always interrupting? That is so lame."

Now, if you were thinking like a behavior analyst, you would be saying to yourself, "I wonder why Kevin does this? It's really rude and irritating for sure, but there must be something that sets him off and I know that something is keeping him going. I've got to be a better observer on this one." You would then approach the next party as though you were an anthropologist observing the rituals of a long-lost tribe of New Guinea. First, you would look for the stimulus that seemed to set the stage for Kevin's interrupting, then, you'd watch closely for anything that seemed to prompt his

> ** Everything you see people do has a cause.**

rude behavior. You would notice that Kevin interrupts when a certain person speaks or when a certain topic comes up. Make a mental note of this and then watch to see what happens right after Kevin finishes his comment; do people laugh, disagree with him, or do something else distinctive? Now notice Kevin's reaction to this event. You may discover he always butts in when the topic turns to something he knows about such as NASCAR racing. He seems to have an encyclopedic memory for races, drivers, records, and sponsors in NASCAR, as well as what seems like an unlimited number of memorized facts about many other topics. He tosses out some little-known fact and then gets a satisfied look on his face when everyone looks bewildered and the conversation stops for a minute. Sometimes someone will groan, at other times someone blurts out, "Really? And how do you happen know that, Kevin?" at which point he gets to tell a story that usually has no relevance whatsoever.

So, to deal with a person like Kevin effectively, you have to observe closely and determine how and when his obnoxious behaviors are reinforced by the people around him. This is how a behavior analyst thinks—objectively, analytically, cause and effect: stimulus > behavior > consequence. Everything you see people do has a cause. When you understand this, you'll be able to manage people like Kevin by ignoring obnoxious behaviors and reinforcing behaviors that are socially acceptable.

The notion that behavior analysts care about the cause of behavior may be new to some people. Back in the beginning (mid-1960s), our field was called *behavior modification*. At that time the predominant thinking was, "We don't care what the cause of the behavior is, we just want to fix it." This emphasis led to an unfortunate strategy: Discover and demonstrate the effective use of aversive consequences to suppress or eliminate behavior.

In 1982, things changed significantly when a pivotal study was published clearly demonstrating that it was possible to find controlling variables for severe behavior problems and use this information to develop effective treatments (Iwata, Dorsey, Slifer, Bauman, & Richman, 1982). In this study, Brian Iwata and other researchers at The Johns Hopkins University School of Medicine and the John F. Kennedy Institute in Baltimore worked with children who engaged in severe self-injury. Self-injury is one of the most perplexing behaviors imaginable. Examples of self-injury include children or adults who bang their heads, scratch or bite themselves, pull out their own hair, or gouge their own eyes. When the causes (such as attention or escaping demands) of the self-injury were identified, it was possible to effectively treat the behaviors.

Since the 1982 Iwata et al. study, it has been accepted as a best practice for behavior analysts not only to take a *baseline* (measurement before treatment) but also to perform a *functional assessment* prior to the onset of treatment. Some common "functions" that have been isolated include adult attention, escape from aversive stimuli, access to tangible reinforcers, and pure, automatic self-stimulation. Each functional analysis is performed in a standard way, but the variables tested are unique to each individual assessed and they can reveal some surprising results. A severe and dangerous behavior such as self-injury or aggression might be maintained by escape from an instructional or demand situation or it might be maintained by accidental attention from a staff member or even a parent. Finding the cause of a behavior means that the behavior analyst can develop the most effective and humane treatment possible.

"Finding the cause of a behavior means that the behavior analyst can develop the most effective and humane treatment possible."

In the course of conducting a functional analysis, we are sometimes surprised by what we find. A teacher, complaining to the school behavior analyst about a 5th grader who is constantly out of his seat in math class, may want a more effective punisher to make him settle down. "I've tried making him face the wall, I've tried taking away privileges, I've threatened to call his father—nothing seems to work," reports his teacher. Using a functional assessment, however, may reveal that the "cause" of the out-of-seat behavior is actually classroom work that is simply too difficult for this student. Our very mobile, roving 5th grader may be unable to say, "Look, this stuff is too hard for me, and it's frustrating to try and do these problems. I think I'll just take a break and go sharpen my pencil, and while I'm at it, visit with my friend Mark across the room. It won't take long." But, little Johnny Mobile just can't find the words, and knows that he would be punished if he complained about the work. Many of us have heard far less than desirable solutions, such as the following reaction to problems in classrooms: "You think the problems are too hard? And you think you need a break? Life is hard, young man. Now get back to work." Clearly, if we knew changing the curriculum would eliminate the wandering and out-of-seat behavior, it would be far more humane to change young Mr. Mobile's math exercises than to punish him for this perfectly understandable behavior.

Another meaning of *analyze* is to demonstrate *experimental control* (Baer, Wolf, & Risley, 1968). In the Dicky study described in Question 1, Wolf et al. (1964) analyzed the effect of the time-out procedure by showing systematically that when 10 minutes of time-out followed glasses throwing, the throwing was reduced to zero in 5 days. When the contingency was dropped for 3 weeks, glasses throwing went back up to the previous level; reinstituting the time-out procedure again reduced the glasses throwing to zero, this time in only 6 days.

Functional assessments are conducted by responsible behavior analysts before a treatment is implemented.

Exhibit 1 shows how a graph provides a visual representation that can help us analyze data.

So, in summary, behavior analysis is just what the name says. It involves analyzing behavior by identifying maintaining variables. Functional analysis is used to determine the conditions under which a behavior is likely to occur. Functional assessments are conducted by responsible behavior analysts *before* a treatment is implemented.

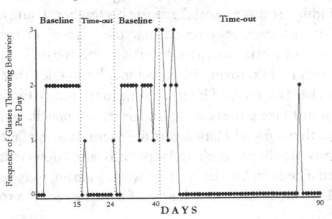

EXHIBIT 1. Dicky's glasses throwing behavior was reduced using a time-out procedure.

●●●

Key Concepts:

Behavior analysts analyze behavior, take baseline data, consider maintaining variables, conduct functional analyses, and work to achieve experimental control.

EXERCISES:

1. Take note of some behavior of a person you encounter regularly who has an unusual or annoying behavior.
2. Try to figure out what the stimulus is for the behavior and what might be maintaining it. However, we don't suggest that you try to change the behavior at this point.

QUESTION #3.

Is behavior analysis a science or is it just another form of clinical treatment?

Behavior analysis is a technology based on the science of behavior. Applied behavior analysis is a way of thinking about the many different aspects of human behavior and then devising scientifically based treatments that are practical and useful. As you have already seen, behavior analysts are primarily interested in making clinically significant changes in socially important, observable behaviors of individuals who need assistance with behavior problems. Behavior analysts deal almost entirely with learned behaviors and we work hard to ensure improvements in behavior will generalize to all of the important settings in the person's life.

> **"... behavior analysts are primarily interested in making clinically significant changes in socially important, observable behaviors of individuals who need assistance with behavior problems."**

The primary goals of behavioral treatment are: (a) to help people improve their lives by gaining skills so they can become more independent and, (b) to reduce or eliminate behaviors that cause individuals to receive various forms of rejection, abuse, or punishment from others. Behavior analysts believe that the primary controlling variables in a person's life reside in the physical and social environment and reinforcement is a central concept in the understanding of human behavior. We believe as a general rule, if a desirable behavior is not occurring, it is probably because there is no reinforcement available to sustain it. We also know from the past several decades of applied research when the natural environment is full of punishers, both natural and man-made, certain behaviors can be suppressed and this is sometimes a desirable outcome. Placing one's hand on a hot stove and getting burned is a natural punisher that will hopefully result in the desirable outcome of avoiding the touching of hot stoves in the future.

As shown in the case of Dicky, as behavior analysts, we think analytically; we look for cause–effect relationships in the environment, and we try to show some sort of demonstration of experimental control to make sure the change in behavior we produced was not due to chance or some other outside variable.

Most behavior analysts think visually about the behaviors on which they are working. We operate like committed scientists part of the time and like caring clinicians the rest of the time. When we are operating like scientists, we are defining the behavior we are working on very precisely, we *take data continuously,* and we graph the data so we can do a *visual analysis* that allows us to see trends in performance over time. As we do our interventions, we *evaluate the results.* This means we continue to take data to make sure that the intervention is working. If the data show an intervention is not working (e.g., the person is not improving) we make midcourse corrections to find something that will work.

Here's a typical example of a behavior that might be addressed by a behavior analyst. Marge, a supervisor, reports that the developmentally disabled adults in her group home do not take responsibility for completing some of the chores that need to be done each day. The behavior analyst would start by asking Marge to define the tasks carefully. Then Marge would be asked to take some data for a few days to make sure that a problem actually existed. These data would be graphed, as shown in

> **"We operate like committed scientists part of the time and like caring clinicians the rest of the time."**

Exhibit 2. Because it looks like there is a significant problem, the behavior analysts asks Marge a series of questions and determines that she is not consistent in praising the clients for their work. The behavior analyst writes a behavior program that involves having Marge consistently praise the completion of tasks done by the clients. Most people would think this is a good idea and that this intervention would probably work just fine. Our behavior analyst wants to know for sure if the intervention is effective, so she continues to graph the data. Oops, it looks like the praise was not quite enough to change this behavior. A second look at the problem of completing the chores shows the clients would rather spend time watching TV than taking out the trash, vacuuming the living room, or helping set the table for dinner. Marge and the behavior analyst put their heads together again and decide to use a behavioral technique called the *Premack Principle.*[3] Basically this involves setting up the rules in the house so that the preferred behavior (watching TV) is used as a reinforcer for the nonpreferred behavior (helping with chores). Marge essentially says, "No TV until chores are done." We can see that this really gets the attention of the clients who quickly volunteer to help out so they can watch *Judge Judy,* one of their favorite late afternoon shows. A good behavior analyst will also want to follow up to ensure the modified behavior plan is working. Follow-up is the last phase of our informal study. When the behavior analyst is confident that Marge can effectively implement the program revision

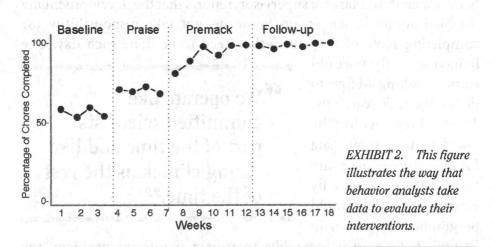

EXHIBIT 2. This figure illustrates the way that behavior analysts take data to evaluate their interventions.

---

[3]The Premack Principle is named after Dr. David Premack (1965), who made the observation that high-probability behaviors could be used as reinforcers for low-probability behaviors.

involving the Premack Principle, she moves on to help other people with their behavior management problems.

● ●

Key Concepts:

Behavior analysis involves continuous data collection, visual analysis, and ongoing evaluation of results. You might think of it as a way of finding the "cause" of a particular behavior. The Premack Principle is a procedure that can be used to change behavior.

EXERCISES:

1. Select a behavior you can observe every day. This can be one of your own behaviors you are trying to change. Define the behavior precisely, count it, and when you have a few days of data, graph the data to determine what they show.

2. Look for an article in the *Journal of Applied Behavior Analysis* on a specific behavior that interests you and examine the graphs closely. Can you see any variability in the data? Do you see any trending? Notice where the condition lines separating each intervention are drawn. Can you determine if the intervention made a significant difference in the behavior?

QUESTION #4.

What exactly is *evidence-based treatment?* Isn't there evidence for all treatments?

In the summer of 2003, it was a hot, muggy Saturday evening in Milwaukee when an 8-year-old boy with "violent tendencies" met his death at the hands of church leaders. These trusted religious authorities were trying to rid this innocent child of the demons they believed to be the cause of his strange and unpredictable behaviors. And although these well intended, God-fearing souls certainly did not intend to murder this little boy, by using a "treatment" with no basis whatsoever in any clinical or behavioral research literature, they essentially sentenced him to death.

Although it may seem bizarre, this was not the first or only time children have been innocent victims of misguided, uninformed adults who have no knowledge of or comprehension of the concept of *evidence-based treatment.* This term, which is also known as *empirically validated therapies,* refers to a fairly recent awareness (mid-1990s) by therapeutic professionals that the time has come to pass judgment on those treatments that cannot stand up to scientific scrutiny. It is simply no longer tolerable for pseudoprofessionals who offer miracle cures to be allowed to practice their craft at the expense of naïve and trusting citizens.

> **"Behavior analysts are pleased to point out that our procedures have been evidence-based since the beginning of the field in the mid-1960s."**

One such therapy is "water-intoxication," which supposedly will promote bonding in children with "attachment disorder." On the advice of counselors at a treatment center in Utah, the parents of a 4-year-old girl forced her to drink so much water it lowered the concentration of sodium in her blood, causing fatal brain swelling.

Needless to say, water-intoxication is not an evidence-based treatment; it is based entirely on a counterintuitive, theoretical notion called "paradoxical interventions" that will supposedly discourage unwanted behavior and cause children to draw closer to their adoptive parents.

Behavior analysts are pleased to point out that our procedures have been evidence-based since the beginning of the field in the mid-1960s. Behavior analysts always work with specific, defined behaviors, as opposed to "symptoms" or interpretations of behavior. We take data before the treatment is instituted to give us a baseline that is used for comparison with later conditions. And, *experimental control* is demonstrated to clearly show it was the treatment that was the cause of the subsequent behavior change. Behavior analysis is unique in this respect, and as a result of many years of evidence-based, applied research, we can point to the development of highly effective treatments that are safe and dependable.

Behavior analysts think all therapies should adopt some similar sort of accountability system so that consumers can be informed of the effectiveness of the treatment. In our field, we actually have two levels of empirical validation. The first is internal ,where the behavior analyst, as indicated earlier, designs the treatment in such a way that effects can be seen directly by examining the graphs of the data. The second method, called *social validation,* involves including the consumer in the process to make a judgment about the importance of the treatment effect. We basically employ the consumer as the ultimate judge of effectiveness. If clients (or their guardians) can't see the effect, then we would conclude our intervention was not sufficient and it would be back to the drawing boards to devise a better treatment. Other approaches to behavior change do not focus on outcomes that are measurable, in any practical sense, by the consumer. So-called "ropes courses," for example, involve corporate executive and middle managers leaving the office and spending a day or two in a remote setting, where they climb trees, fall and catch each other, and generally engage in "team-building" exercises. The primary form of evaluation is not whether there are measurable improvements in productivity back at the office but rather whether the participants found the experience fun and interesting. By avoiding mention of any tangible effects that transfer back to the office, this approach escapes close scrutiny based on actual outcomes. We would not include these outdoor experiences as a form of evidence-based treatment for workplace productivity even if they are well liked by one and all.

• •

Key Concepts:
Behavior analysis uses: evidence-based treatment, experimental control, and social validation.

EXERCISES:

1. Find an article in the *Journal of Applied Behavior Analysis* that addresses social validation and examine the methods used to involve consumers in the determination of treatment effectiveness.
2. Find an article that does not employ social validation and describe a way to apply this procedure.

QUESTION #5.

Who provides direct behavior-based services?

The short answer is, it depends. Clinical treatments are sometimes carried out by direct-care staff who have been specially trained, teacher aides, behavioral assistants, parents, or in some cases, the treatment is actually done by a Board Certified Behavior Analyst™ until others are adequately trained. When behavior analysis is used in business and industry settings, the behavior analyst will usually train supervisors and managers to carry out the interventions and department heads to monitor and provide graphic feedback.

Remember Dicky, the autistic child, and his severe behavior problems? Do you recall the treatment that was used? The analysis of his outrageous, out-of-control, self-injurious behaviors showed the behaviors were maintained by attention, primarily from his mother, who was the most central figure in his life at that time. Imagine having cataracts removed at the age of 2 and how strange and scary the world must have seemed to helpless little Dicky. Now combine this with possible brain damage and some degree of mental retardation and you've got a potent mix that would present a challenge to even the most experienced professional. Mom was under tremendous pressure because she was told if Dicky did not begin wearing corrective glasses in the next few months he might lose his vision entirely. Naturally, when Dicky resisted, mom backed off, a very natural reaction. She must have thought, "I can see that this is uncomfortable for him, I'll try later when he calms down. Maybe if I just hold him for a while he'll be ready to try them later." Such actions on the part of a mother dealing with a difficult child are completely understandable. In Dicky's case, over the next several months, his mother's behavior essentially reinforced Dicky for increasingly extreme tantrums until he was completely unmanageable. Consider the setting for Dicky's problems—at home, where his surroundings set the occasion for the violent head banging, hair pulling, and face scratching. What our behavioral experts Wolf, Risley, and Mees (1964) concluded was Dicky needed a different environment and a new person—someone with no *history of reinforcement*—to provide his treatment for the next few months. You may have also noticed the actual treatment was not carried out by these pioneering behavior analysts, but rather by "attendants"— regular day-shift employees of the hospital. Although we don't know for sure, they probably did not even have college degrees (these are generally entry-level positions that pay minimum wage salaries). Mont Wolf and his colleagues carefully analyzed Dicky's behavior problems, wrote out a set of instructions for the attendants to follow, and then closely monitored the results. The treatment itself consisted of the use of time-out (a mild punisher) *contingent on* severe tantrums and then positive reinforcement when his tantrums stopped (i.e., he was returned to the hospital ward). This simple plan could be carried out throughout the day by those attendants on duty at the time. The attendants would carry out the program when necessary and record when Dicky went into time-out and when he came out. After 1 month of treatment Dicky's parents were allowed a 1-hour visit, "… during which an attendant observed and instructed them in their handling of Dicky." This model of treatment has become the norm for our field: an expert in behavior analysis observes the client, takes some baseline data, looks closely at the contingencies of reinforcement that are in play at the time, prepares a written behavior plan, and then trains the normal caregivers (in this case, the attendants) to carry out the program. All of the dramatic results that were seen in this little autistic boy's behavior were entirely produced by entry-level hospital ward employees and by the parents who were trained by those very same staff.[4]

Whereas in many other forms of therapy a child might see a therapist at most three times per week, Dicky received behavioral treatment 24 hours a day, 7 days a week, by staff who were trained by the experts. Soon after the publication of this remarkable case study, the model was further strengthened by two other behavioral experts. Tharp and Wetzel (1969) described the *triadic model*, one in which a consultant

---

[4]Wolf, Risley, and Mees (1964) do describe their only direct contact with Dicky, which occurred during the 5th week of treatment: The shaping program to get him to wear his glasses was not going well, "… so the authors, who had not previously spent any time shaping the subject themselves, spent the major portion of a day directing the shaping procedure."

directs a mediator (in this case, the attendants) to intervene with a "target" (in this case, Dicky).

This method of intervention makes the most sense given the assumptions of the overall behavioral model. If we are working with learned behaviors that are maintained by contingencies in the natural environment, it only makes sense that those people that are in contact with the child the most will have to intervene. This most likely involves changing their behavior because they are very likely to be major players in the maintenance of the behavior problem. The child is the primary focus, of course, but without involving the mediators it would be impossible to make any significant change in the child's behavior. The traditional model of therapy would suggest that the child needs treatment, so he or she goes to see the child psychologist once a week; behavior analysis treats the behavior where the problem occurs and trains the significant parties as essentially para-professional therapists. In the study with Dicky, because more control over the contingencies was necessary, treatment was moved to the hospital and the parents were trained to work with him at home a few months later. With a less severe case, the behavior analyst would go into the home observe and analyze the situation (including the contingencies) and train the parents directly in the home setting. In school settings, if a teacher refers a student with a serious behavior problem, the

"Behavior analysis treats the behavior where the problem occurs."

behavior analyst will come into the classroom, size up the situation, and then train the teacher to be the intervention agent.

Likewise, in a corporate environment, the performance management consultant will usually be brought in by the CEO, who is looking for some new strategies to improve quality or productivity or to reduce accidents and injuries. Because the consultant has no authority over the employees, he or she will need to find and train key supervisors and managers who do have the authority and who are motivated to apply the principles of behavior in the workplace. Countless studies have shown that using the triadic model in business and industry can increase productivity, improve safety, and enhance the quality of service. Most employees want to be more effective, but it is management's job to find a way to properly give feedback and design compensation systems that will motivate employees on a daily basis. This is accomplished through existing supervisory personnel who are guided by an expert in behavior analysis.

> **"Countless studies have shown that using the triadic model in business and industry can increase productivity, improve safety, and enhance the quality of service."**

Key Concepts:

Behavior analysts consider an individual's history of reinforcement. Contingencies are used to change behavior. Contingencies involve behaviors that are contingent on reinforcers. The Triadic Model is used in behavior analysis consulting. This model has a consultant who directs a mediator on how to intervene with a "target" client or consumer.

EXERCISES:

1. Find a setting where you can make some informal observations without being obtrusive (e.g., your local mall, a park) and observe to see if you can find a mediator whose behavior is maintaining an inappropriate behavior. You should simply observe and you should not try to intervene.
2. Think about the study with Dicky, the autistic child. What changes could be made by the mediator you observed to change the behavior of your target?

QUESTION #6.
Is behavior really all that predictable?

This is really a good question and one that we hear all the time from people outside the field of behavior analysis. The brief answer is behavior, for the most part, is very predictable. The longer answer involves an examination of what *prediction* involves and how accurate the prediction is expected to be. Here are a couple of general observations that we can start with: First, the best predictor of future behavior is past behavior.[5] Second, the more information we have about a person, the

> **"The best predictor of future behavior is past behavior."**

behavior we are trying to predict, and the circumstances under which the behavior occurs, the better our prediction will be. In behavior analysis we do a lot of predicting, because that is our business, so to speak. We have some special techniques that we use to assist us with the prediction of future behavior.

We begin by having a fairly precise definition of the behavior we are studying. We initially look at behavior *topographically*, that is, the form of the behavior. For example, if we were studying self-injurious behavior of a young boy, we would look at whether the behavior was head banging, face scratching, or some other specific behavior. We would define the behavior in terms of the position of the child's hand, whether or not he made a fist, how fast the movement occurred, and whether or not it appeared to be forceful. The second way we look at behavior is functionally, that is, regardless of the form of the behavior, what effect did it have? What seemed to be produced by the behavior? What effect did it have on the physical or social environment?

---

[5]This expression does not have an original author who can be cited at this time, although Edwin Guthrie (1944, p. 62) comes the closest to expressing this idea.

If one of our severely developmentally disabled clients hits his head, what do the staff or house parents do? Does he get his way? Does he get out of doing something? Do people come running and feel sorry for him? The more we know about the result of the behavior, the better we are at predicting when he will do it next. As a matter of fact, one of the principal tools behavior analysts use is a *functional analysis*. This is where we test various consequences to see which appear to be maintaining the behavior. If we can find the right consequence, we can get to the point we can predict behavior with pretty good accuracy. Once a conclusion is reached, the likely "cause" can be tested in a controlled or natural setting to determine if the functional analysis was valid.

In behavior analysis we want to be able to predict behavior so we can determine whether a certain change in the environment had an effect on the behavior. In our baseline, as shown in Exhibit 3, we are predicting that if nothing changes, the behavior will continue to occur at about the same rate. By changing the environment in some way, we want to change the direction of the behavior and predict that if we keep the change in place, the behavior will continue in the same way. As shown in the exhibit, there is an increasing rate of occurrence of the head banging, and we would predict it will continue headed in an upward direction unless something is done. Now let's add a contingency to the environment that states, "Play music as long as he's not head banging; if he starts, turn it off for at least 5 minutes." You can see that the music changes the direction of the behavior and there is a clear *downtrend*. The behavior is still predictable, however.

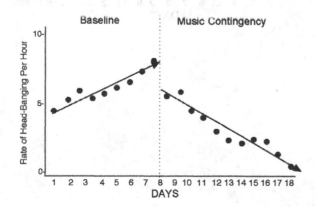

EXHIBIT 3. *We are predicting the behavior will continue increasing unless something is done. The intervention seems to produce a change in direction but the behavior is still predictable.*

> **"Before we can do anything about changing a behavior we have to be able to predict it."**

Before we can do anything about changing a behavior we have to be able to predict it. If the baseline condition were variable, as shown in Exhibit 4, it would be impossible to determine whether the intervention had any effect.

So, the answer to the question "Is behavior really all that predictable?" is, if we have enough of the right kind of information, behavior is very predictable. Behavior analysts use prediction as part of our analysis of behavior and attempt as much as possible to use scientific means to predict what people are going to do. Then we try to predict the effects of certain treatments so we can help people change their behaviors and improve their lives.

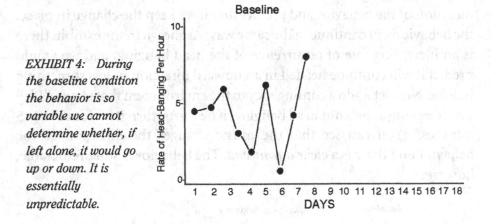

Baseline

EXHIBIT 4: During the baseline condition the behavior is so variable we cannot determine whether, if left alone, it would go up or down. It is essentially unpredictable.

● ●

Key Concepts:

Behavior analytic concepts related to evaluating data include predictability, topography, function, variability, and trending.

EXERCISES:

1. If you have access to a setting where you can make some unobtrusive observations of behavior, observe and try to predict what a person is going to do next.
2. Graph the frequency of the behavior over time and try to predict the behavior from day to day.

QUESTION #7.
So, behavior analysts don't have theories, they just have data?

You may recall from Question 4 the story of the 4-year-old girl who died from water-intoxication therapy; the excessive water was administered by her parents at the advice of counselors who had their own theory for "attachment disordered" children. This *theory* suggested paradoxical interventions such as this would discourage inappropriate behavior and would somehow cause the little girl to draw closer to her parents. It is this sort of reckless theorizing behavior analysts find totally abhorrent and that reinforces their conviction that we are simply better off without theories.

This is not to say we don't have guesses, hunches, or ideas about how the environment affects human behavior; we do. But our speculations are tightly bound to the experiments being conducted and it is rare that you will hear of any grand theory coming from a behavior analyst. Although we might be interested in understanding "attachment" (the enduring social emotional relationship between a child and a parent; Zimbardo, Johnson, & Weber, 2006), having such a description or a theory about how it is formed is unlikely to help us improve the relationship between a specific child that we are treating and her parents, who are desperately seeking answers. We are not saying other researchers shouldn't pursue such lines of inquiry, but rather this is not the tradition of applied behavior analysis, where we have more immediate and pressing objectives.

For a child who is not bonding with her parents, we would first want to know what types of behaviors are of concern to the parents. These might include failure to make eye contact; a propensity for lying and stealing; and possibly even animal cruelty, starting fires, or other antisocial behaviors. Using our *theory of behavior* (Skinner, 1953, 1969) we would analyze each behavior to determine what the controlling variables were. We would then set out a course of treatment for the parents whereby each behavior would be increased or decreased as desired. Nowadays the treatment would probably not take place in a treatment center but rather in the setting where the controlling variables were operating. The behavior analyst would most likely spend many hours working with the parents in their home, teaching them the skills they would need, demonstrating special procedures and

> **"It is possible to determine for individual subjects procedures that can be used to quickly change behavior, and those changes can be maintained over a considerable period of time."**

reinforcing them for behavior improvements shown by their child. Hundreds of studies have been conducted on behaviors such as these over the past 4 decades and a workable technology of parent training is well understood at this time (Wahler, Vigilante, & Strand, 2004).

One early study (Wahler, 1969) illustrates this strategy quite nicely. Dr. Robert Wahler, a professor at the University of Tennessee, and his assistants worked with two families who both had elementary school-age boys who were described as, "stubborn," "negativistic," and "headstrong." Observations were made in the homes of the children. As shown in Exhibit 5, Billy engaged in 100 to nearly 200 oppositional "units" of behavior in the 40-minute periods set aside for observational purposes. Wahler then analyzed the troubling behavior and concluded the parents offered little in the way of negative consequences for not following requests. In addition, he found their attention might not be all that reinforcing. He trained the parents to use time-out and differential reinforcement.[6] As Exhibit 5 also shows, when the Time-out and Differential Reinforcement condition was in place, the oppositional behavior dropped to near zero in only 5 weeks. This is quite dramatic,

---

[6]*Differential reinforcement* involves following only some selected behaviors with a preselected reinforcer; this is also called *shaping* or *behavior shaping*.

because Billy had demonstrated oppositional behavior for many months prior to treatment. As is common in this type of single-subject design research, Wahler returned to the Baseline condition (the parents quit using time-out and differential reinforcement) to determine if the behavior would reverse. You can see that the behavior did reverse very quickly over the next 2 weeks. When the parents again instituted the time-out and differential reinforcement, the troublesome oppositional behavior dropped quickly to zero and remained there for over 2 months. This study exemplifies how our behavior theory works in practice. It is possible to determine for individual subjects procedures that can be used to quickly change behavior and those changes can be maintained over a considerable period of time.

Not having a separate theory for each and every type of behavior has not been a limitation to the field of behavior analysis. Our basic and applied researchers have been quite productive over the past 50 years, developing effective interventions based on B.F. Skinner's original theory of behavior (Skinner, 1938). This includes not only behavior therapy for deviant child behavior and parent training, but also effective treatments for classrooms, residential facilities, sheltered workshops, business and industrial sites, and, most recently, executive coaching for CEOs of major corporations. Behavior analysis is a thriving, innovative field of productive basic and applied researchers and therapists who all derive

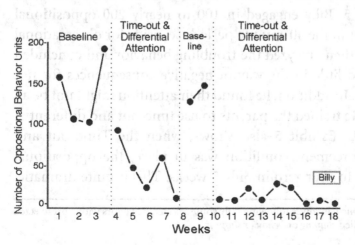

EXHIBIT 5. (after Wahler, 1969) shows the effects of Time-out and Differential Reinforcement on Billy's oppositional behavior in weekly observational sessions over a 20-week period.

their inspiration from one basic theory. Behavior analysts are motivated to expand and apply their knowledge primarily by the creative application of *data-based* approaches rather than theory testing.

> **"Not having a separate theory for each and every type of behavior has not been a limitation to the field of behavior analysis."**

• •

Key Concepts:
Rather than focus on theory, theories of behavior, and other similar concepts, behavior analysis is data based.

EXERCISES:

1. Think of some behavior-related topic that you find of interest and explore the search engine of the *Journal of Applied Behavior Analysis* to find studies that are relevant.
2. Look at the *Journal of Applied Behavior Analysis* studies available at http//:seab.envmed.rochester.edu/jaba/ to determine if the authors engaged in the research because they were motivated by any particular theories.

SUMMARY OF BASIC CONCEPTS

Behavior analysts think about human behavior differently than do most other human service professionals. We focus on the actual behavior as it is presented, rather than looking at the behavior as a symptom of some deeper, underlying problem. We assume that these observed behaviors are learned and are maintained in the individual's natural environment. Although we are often presented with complex behavioral issues of unknown origin, our strategy is always to use data and proceed systematically.

TOP TEN TASKS LIST
FOR BEHAVIOR ANALYSTS

1. Define the behavior objectively.
2. Set up a data collection system.
3. Gather enough data to determine how serious the problem is.
4. Graph the data. (Determine the pattern of the behavior over time/stability of the behavior.)
5. Conduct a functional analysis. (Determine the controlling variables for the behavior.)
6. Use the results of the functional assessment (along with other information from interviews and informal observations; if needed, do a search of the research literature to determine what previous treatments have proven successful).
7. Develop a treatment plan.
8. Identify the mediator and train that person to implement the treatment plan.
9. Demonstrate the treatment plan, make sure it works, and then train others such as the parents, teacher, or supervisor.
10. Collect data throughout this process so that the effects of the treatment can be evaluated.

The behavior analyst is looking for socially significant behavior changes that are sizeable enough to make an important difference in a person's life as well as improve the quality of the person's life to a significant degree. When possible, the behavior analyst employs a research design that demonstrates it was indeed the treatment that produced the effect and not some outside variable.

The typical behavior analyst is part clinician, part detective, and part scientist. Behavior analysts are often client advocates who will try to obtain services for clients to improve their quality of life. A behavior analyst thinks of normal and abnormal behavior as being at two ends of a continuum, where both are learned by the same principles of behavior. Abnormal behavior may be maladaptive or self-injurious, destructive, or dangerous, but our view is it is all learned and can

> **"A behavior analyst thinks of normal and abnormal behavior as being at two ends of a continuum, where both are learned by the same principles of behavior."**

be reduced and a replacement behavior can be found, taught to the individual, and maintained by new contingencies of reinforcement. A child or adult who is oppositional is a person who doesn't respond to requests that are made. Such responses can be taught and oppositional behaviors can be put on extinction so that they are no longer reinforced. The antisocial person is one who engages in inappropriate behaviors. These behaviors can likely be replaced with more socially appropriate behaviors by a careful rearrangement of the contingencies of reinforcement that surround the behaviors.

All of this is routinely accomplished without the need for elaborate theories of personality, memory, motivation, or development. Behavior analysts have one core set of behavior principles (Michael, 1993) and these can be applied in a wide variety of settings to help people of all ages and functioning levels.

> "A behavior analyst thinks of normal and abnormal behavior as being at two ends of a continuum, where both are learned by the same principles of behavior."

Chapter

Two

Applications

QUESTION #8.
Can you use behavior analysis in "real life"?

Behavior analysis principles can be applied directly in real life, every day, for the benefit of everyone. For example, a teacher who has a thorough understanding of behavior principles can motivate her students to stay on task, improve their academic performance, and gain significant interpersonal skills in dealing with peers. Many teachers face unruly, acting-out, belligerent, and aggressive children on a day-to-day basis. Those

> **"Behavior analysis principles can be applied directly in real life, every day, for the benefit of everyone."**

who understand the basic principles of classroom management derived from behavior analysis will know how to use extinction with attention-maintained behaviors and when to reinforce approximations to appropriate behavior (shaping). A behaviorally trained teacher understands the power of attention as a reinforcer; she knows that looking at a child, smiling, and giving even the slightest praise can strengthen specific behaviors. A well trained teacher uses this strategy every minute of the day, constantly looking for behavior to reinforce and systematically ignoring any inappropriate classroom behavior.

Teachers who are well versed in behavior analysis also know when to call for help from a behavior analyst. In tough cases, the behavior analysts will conduct a functional assessment to determine the controlling variables of the behavior. The behavior analyst might also guide teachers through the implementation of more powerful classroom management systems such as individualized behavior programs, The Good Behavior Game, classroom token economies, and the use of time-out and response-cost procedures (Sulzer-Azaroff & Mayer, 1991). In short, when behavior analysis is used in the classroom, teachers stand to benefit significantly, with increased peace of mind, knowing that the classroom is under control and students are motivated by the consistent, contingent, effective use of reinforcement. These are teachers who never have to raise their voices or use threatening gestures or remarks.

Parents also benefit greatly from the use of the principles of behavior in their moment-to-moment management of their children. Behavior analysis can help parents end the chaos that often accompanies simple daily routines such as, "It's time to get dressed for school. Hurry, or you'll miss your bus." or, "Okay, bed time. Let's put away those toys and get your pajamas on; we've got a full day tomorrow."

> **" Parents also benefit greatly from the use of the principles of behavior in their moment-to-moment management of their children. "**

Young children adore their parents, and even the slightest attention is a powerful reinforcer. In addition, parents control all the reinforcers in a child's life—from privileges such as staying up late, to permissions to go outside or play a video game, to gifts that these days can be quite lavish. Considering this, the mistake many parents make is that they do not make these reinforcers contingent on good behavior. Instead, they give them out noncontingently—or worse, they unknowingly reward a child's inappropriate or manipulative behaviors. Consider the following all-too-common interchange:

> *"Rudy, it's time to go to bed." "No, I want to play with my dinosaurs." "Rudy, don't talk back to me. I said it's time to go to bed." "No, no, it's not fair! Just a little more time? Please, you ALWAYS do this to me, mom!" "Okay, Rudy. I'm sorry. Hurry up and finish playing with your toys, then go to bed. Please, Rudy, mom's tired. I'm sorry, but you just have to learn to go to bed."*

This mom has no clue she has just reinforced some very problematic behavior that will come to haunt her in the very near future. Rudy has learned he doesn't have to listen to his mom, he can cajole and threaten, then whine and plead and get his way. A parent well trained in basic principles would be far better equipped to handle this situation. She would know you don't give instructions and then fail to follow through, because it is essentially teaching the child he or she doesn't need to follow instructions. And, of course, she is training little Rudy that making accusatory remarks can buy him a few more minutes of time with his beloved Brontosaurus, a very powerful reinforcer indeed. Although she's not a behavior analyst, this mom has accidentally used the principles to shape bad behavior. If she continues with this, Rudy will become more and more noncompliant as he gets older, and at some point she will most likely find herself getting angry and using punishment with an out-of-control teenager: "Okay, Rudy. Young man, you are on restriction for the rest of the week; no phone, no TV, and no video games. And I mean it this time!" When this fails, she'll seek counseling for her now-rebellious teen—who may pick up the label "oppositional defiant disorder"—and if counseling doesn't prove effective, the next step is medication—or maybe Rudy will be shipped off to a class for behavioral needs students or military school to "teach him some discipline."

Another persistent example is that of the "lazy" employee. Many supervisors complain their employees will do what they are told, but then they just sit and wait for further instructions. What the supervisor would like to see is a worker who shows some initiative, who informs the boss when work is complete, and who asks, "What else can I do to help out?" The question a behavior analyst would ask about a pervasive motivation problem is this: What prompts exist for this behavior and what reinforcers are available to someone who does ask for extra work or who just takes on additional tasks without any prompting? In most cases there are *no* rewards for showing initiative and, basically, the work environment needs to be specially designed so taking on new tasks is heavily rewarded.

● ●

Key Concepts:
Shaping

EXERCISES

1. Keep a diary of your own daily activities for a week and make note of behaviors you would like to improve. Maybe you want to quit smoking, lose some weight, get more exercise, or maybe study for exams more effectively. Then, try to think like a behavior analyst and determine if there is some way to improve your own behavior. For example, you might try the Premack Principle and make a list of reinforcing activities you enjoy and a second list of behaviors you need to accomplish. Then, pair each desired behavior with a reinforcing event. Write a contract for yourself that says something like: "If I get my term paper done by Friday noon, I will go out and party with my friends on Friday night." Try this form of managing one of your own behavior problems for a few weeks and see if you find yourself feeling more in control, getting more done, and enjoying your reinforcing activities more.

   If you are not successful because you are great at talking yourself out of doing what you don't like to do, can you think of methods that could be used to get your behavior under control?

2. Keep a diary of your own daily activities for a week and make note of frustrating situations you might encounter with others. Then, try to analyze one of them as you try to think like a behavior analyst and see if you can see how you might have handled the situation differently to produce a different, less stressful result.

QUESTION #9.

Can I use behavioral procedures to help me improve my own behavior or enhance my performance?

Absolutely. For the behavior analyst, "behavior change begins at home" is a commonly accepted value. We take seriously the notion that professionals in this field should "walk the walk," not just "talk the talk." By analyzing their own behavior, specialists in this new technology can not only model for others how behavior change can

> **"For the behavior analyst, "behavior change begins at home" is a commonly accepted value."**

be done, but they can also gain some sense of how difficult it can be to change behavior. As a behavior analyst, changing one's own problem behaviors will result in a greater understanding of what clients are experiencing.

Skinner himself was a great model of self-management (Epstein, 1997). Because he was so committed to writing, Skinner frequently modified his office space to increase his productivity. To decrease fidgeting, he modified the seat cushion on his chair and he installed timers and invented a "thinking aid" (Skinner, 1987, p. 379) to improve his output. Long before this equipment was common at every gym, to get himself to engage in the unpleasant task of riding his exercise bike, Skinner installed a holder to

> **"It is not enough to live your life ... you also need to analyze it and make changes in it frequently and regularly."**
> (Epstein, 1997)

position reading materials so he could read while improving his cardiovascular fitness. Skinner was pleased that he had developed a theory of behavior that had practical implications: "It is not enough to live your life ... you also need to analyze it and make changes in it frequently and regularly" (Epstein, 1997, p. 559).

You can apply the basic principles yourself to help you lose weight, increase your exercise, stop smoking, study more effectively, improve your public speaking or interpersonal skills. This area of application is generally referred to as *self-management,* and there are a significant number of studies that have been published to establish concrete steps you can take (Miltenberger, 2001). These include defining the target behavior, doing a functional assessment, setting a goal, choosing and implementing the appropriate self-management strategy, and evaluating the change.

Let's say another new year is approaching and this time, by golly, you want to make a resolution to get healthy and actually keep it. We had a friend who joined a gym and 3 months later saw one of the fitness trainers in the grocery store. The trainer said, "I haven't seen you at the gym since the day you joined." Our friend joked, "Oh, I didn't realize I actually had to come there—I thought if I just joined, I'd get healthy." Unlike our friend, this year, you're determined to go to the gym, lose that extra 25 pounds, and get scores on your annual physical exam that will make your doctor smile. You've identified the target behaviors: to go to the gym at least 3 times a week and to lose 25 pounds in 12 months. You should do a functional assessment to determine why you failed before. Is it the time of day you were trying to exercise? If you're not a morning person, trying to go the gym at 5 a.m. before you go to work may not be a good idea. If you have three children who need to be transported to every activity under the sun every day after work, your chauffeur duties may interfere with your

gym time. Is the gym location too far away? You get the idea. Next, think about the consequences. Every time you lose 5 pounds, you could buy yourself a new clothing item, or you could involve your spouse or partner as a support team and go out to a special dinner (within your diet of course). Using a graph with a criterion line will give you a visual picture of how you're doing.

This same approach would be particularly appropriate for the legions of "lone workers" who work at home or, like a UPS driver, must manage their time and schedule their work in the absence of a direct supervisor. Learning to set obtainable objectives, consistently self-monitor, and deliver your own reinforcers contingently is a clear path for success in any job where your boss is not present to supervise you every hour of every day.

As a behavior analyst, you've got the skills to change your own behavior or enhance your own performance. All you need to do is decide you are ready to put an organized plan in place that involves the consistent application of behavioral principles.

• •

Key Concepts:
Self-management

EXERCISES:

1. Choose a personal behavior that you would like to improve.
2. Develop an easy way to count the behavior that you've selected.
3. Now, try to think like a behavior analyst and see if you can figure out what sets the occasion for the behavior or what change you might make to increase the likelihood of the behavior occurring.
4. Implement a change in your behavior and see if you can make an improvement.

QUESTION #10.

My roommate (spouse, boyfriend, child, etc.), is driving me crazy; can any of this help me get along with him?

B ehavioral procedures are ideally suited for changing the behavior of your roommate, friends, in-laws, spouses, or significant others. Frank was a student in one of first author Jon Bailey's psychology classes; he complained in class that his roommate never took out the trash, even though that was one of several chores he had agreed to take on. "He will just walk right by the trash can and head out the door, totally oblivious." After letting him vent for a couple of minutes Bailey said, "Okay, let me see if I have this right. You're saying your roommate should want to take out the trash. ..." Frank nodded, "Yep, I shouldn't have to remind him; it's his responsibility. He agreed to do it." Bailey replied, "A lot of people feel that way about the behavior of others. They think, 'My wife should want to quit smoking,' 'My husband should want to lose weight,' but this kind of thinking is nonproductive. The only place you can go with that is to Blamesville, and I'm not going with you. Blaming people just doesn't work; it does not produce any change in behavior; it just makes you feel good about yourself because you do care about your responsibilities. So, let's move on. How about putting your behavior analyst hat on? Let's look at this problem behaviorally."

Bailey then proceeded to suggest the trash can did not yet have stimulus control over the roommate's behavior. He made the following suggestion, "How about this: take the trash can and put it directly in front of the front door, so that he would have to stumble over it to get out. He'll see it and take out the trash. Now what do you do?" Frank looked puzzled, "Well I don't know, reinforce him?" "Yes, exactly, and then what?" Now Frank was stuck, "Wait till the next day and see what happens?" "Well, you could do that, but it's not the best plan," said Bailey. He then proceeded to remind Frank about stimulus fading—gradually reducing a stimulus that, through manipulation, has gained some control; and continuing this until the environment is back to normal. "So the next day you want me to pull the trash can back just a little bit, is that right?"

"Right, about an inch, and then the next day add another inch—this is going to take a few days; you'll have to be patient." A week later Bailey saw Frank and his roommate at a fundraiser. "Hi, Dr. B. Good to see you here; this is my roommate ..." Before he had a chance to introduce us, the roommate stuck out his hand and said, "Hi, I'm Ben, you know ... the 'trash can guy.' I understand Frank's little experiment was your idea. I thought it was funny. I'm not exactly sure what kind of psychology you teach, but it sure worked, and it was pretty much painless. Basically, Frank got me to break a bad habit without insulting me or ticking me off."

Students and families experience scenarios just like this one all the time. Roommates won't do the dishes; boyfriends or husbands won't pick up their socks. Even behavior analysis graduate students have been so conditioned to complain and get so much pleasure out of being outraged they completely forget to analyze the behavior. And in most cases a simple rearrangement of the environment does the trick—enhancing some stimulus or adding a prompt, shaping small behaviors using immediate, personal reinforcers, and then gradually fading out the extra cues and add-on reinforcers. Changing someone's behavior can be a delicate matter if people think you are trying to manipulate them. Manipulation is a nasty term that suggests you are trying to get something out of a person for your benefit. We would never suggest this practice and push hard for the idea that human relations would be much improved if everyone understood the basic principles of behavior. There is an extremely good chance if you find yourself dealing with uncomfortable situations on a regular basis with a friend, acquaintance, relative, or coworker, you are a part of the problem. You are probably accidentally reinforcing the behavior that is annoying, grating, irritating, or rude.

It is not manipulation to use your reinforcers wisely to produce a behavior that is comfortable for all parties. A recent letter to one of the syndicated self-help columns described a situation where a neighbor would stop over every morning, invite herself in, and suggest, "Why don't we have some coffee and chat?" The columnist advised the letter writer to talk to the neighbor and explain that she is a busy person and doesn't have time for coffee klatching. We object to simplistic recommendations such as this because they do not really deal with the "cause" of the problem. If you think like a behavior analyst about this, you will realize that the neighbor finds the letter writer's conversation reinforcing, and that the best treatment for the behavior is extinction, pure and simple. Basically, we would recommend that after having the conversation (which alone will probably not solve the problem), when the neighbor comes calling again, that the letter writer does not reinforce the behavior. The letter writer could start with telling the neighbor that she really enjoys talking to her, but because she has things to do, such as help a child with homework, it would be very helpful if the neighbor

called first to arrange a time for a visit. If the neighbor doesn't respond to the verbal request, the letter writer can try a different approach. For example, if there is some time during the day that the letter writer is available, she could put a note on the door: "I'm busy until 3 p.m. today. Come over then and we can visit." In this way the letter writer would be selecting an *alternative* or *replacement behavior* that suits her schedule and can reinforce that behavior.

Behavior analysis can help people improve their relationships. With a greater knowledge of human behavior, you can change things for the better.

● ●

Key Concepts:
Stimulus fading, extinction

EXERCISES:

1. If you have a friend or acquaintance who has an annoying behavior, play close attention to the dynamics of your interaction with this friend. Try to determine what the controlling variables (cues) might be for the behavior to occur, and look for the reinforcers. Take some data on the frequency of the behavior.
2. If it turns out that you are reinforcing the behavior, consider making a change. Choose an alternative, acceptable replacement behavior and begin to reinforce that behavior instead.
3. Keep track of the behavior by continuing your frequency count.
4. After 2 weeks, evaluate your personal intervention plan and see if it worked for you.

QUESTION #11.

Why is behavior analysis so popular in the treatment of developmentally disabled individuals?

In the past 100 years, a wide variety of treatments have been used with individuals who have developmental disabilities. Until the 1960s, people with mental retardation and other disabilities were simply left untreated or were "warehoused" in large institutions. In the mid-1960s, some very early applications of behavior modification came on the scene and researchers and practitioners suddenly thought they had a magic cure for retardation. A great deal of good work was done using these early, rather primitive procedures, but there were abuses as well (Bailey & Burch, 2005). Subsequently, an explosion of basic and applied research occurred and continues to this day. Developmentally disabled individuals, through their participation in thousands of studies, have given us a wealth of information about the effectiveness of specific training procedures. We now know how to apply procedures that work with a wide range of behavior problems from severe self-injurious behaviors to methods of training appropriate community and work behaviors.

> **"Behavior analysts by the thousands work with developmentally disabled individuals in a wide variety of settings and there is a constant need for their services."**

Today, applied behavior analysis is considered the most effective treatment modality for almost any behavior problem a developmentally disabled individual might have. The multitude of studies published over the past 3 decades have clearly shown that reinforcers can be used effectively in habilitation so even a severely handicapped person can live a useful and gratifying life in the community. Using contingencies of reinforcement to train and shape adaptive behaviors, people with developmental disabilities can learn useful communication skills so they can express their needs. They can also acquire complex skills such as using public transportation and working in supported-employment positions. Thousands of community-based treatment facilities and residential settings are in place at this time. Parents and teachers as well as professionals and paraprofessionals from many areas have been trained in the basics of behavioral treatment in every state in the United States and in many foreign countries. Behavior analysts by the thousands work with developmentally disabled individuals in a wide variety of settings and there is a constant need for their services. In developmental disabilities settings, behavior analysts are extremely employable all over the United States.

Key Concepts:
Behavioral treatment with the developmentally disabled

EXERCISES:

1. Check with the developmental disability office or with the department of special education in your area to learn what facilities are available.
2. Ask if there is someone you can speak with who provides behavioral treatment. Inquire if this individual will meet with you and help you find a setting where you can observe some ongoing behavioral treatment. Be aware that there may be some issues of confidentiality and you may have to have a background check before you will be allowed to visit a school or community treatment center.

QUESTION #12.

I've read that behavior analysis is used with autistic children too. How do you work with autistic children?

Catherine Maurice was in many ways a typical mother with two small children. A bright, well educated woman whose husband worked on Wall Street, she doted on her two children and had big plans for their futures. Then she noticed something very unusual on her daughter's first birthday. Maurice's precious little girl, Anne-Marie, seemed distant and unattached. Instead of tearing into her presents, she would handle them briefly and then seem to lose interest. Maurice continued observing Anne-Marie, hoping she was just having some bad days. Unfortunately, there were other signs that something was wrong. Maurice remembered that when Anne-Marie was 10 months old, the babysitter had commented that Anne-Marie was such a good little baby and that she "sat and played in one spot for two hours!"[7] In her highly acclaimed book, *Let Me Hear Your Voice: A Family's Triumph Over Autism* (Maurice, 1993), Maurice chronicles the gradual unfolding of her daughter's autistic behavior over several months and her own difficult journey to find effective treatment for Anne-Marie. Maurice's story was especially unusual because her younger child, son Michael, was also diagnosed with autism a few years after Anne-Marie.

In the past 15 years, due to new diagnostic criteria and increases in the services available to children with disabilities, the number of children who have been diagnosed as autistic has dramatically increased. Although there is some reason to doubt that the actual number of autistic children has increased (Gernsbacher, Dawson, & Goldsmith, 2005), what is known is that behavior analytic services for this population are at an all-time high. Although a great deal of money is being poured into basic research on the possible causes of autism, for parents of an autistic child,

---

[7]This book is a must read for anyone interested in effective treatments for autism.

the primary concern is for effective treatment. Sadly, there is a lot of hucksterism associated with this field and it seems almost weekly some new fad or fraud is perpetrated on desperate families who are unable to sort out the fakes from solid and legitimate treatments.

The first peer-reviewed, well controlled, experimental study to be published on the treatment of autism was published in 1987 by Dr. Ivar Lovaas (pronounced LO-voss), a professor on the faculty of the University of California at Los Angeles. This study showed that with intensive one-on-one behavioral treatment (25–40 hours per week), about half of the children in the study appeared to actually recover from autism. Since then, there have been many, many other approaches taken, but none has had anywhere near the degree of scientific replication. At this point we don't know what causes autistic behavior, but we do know how to treat it, and we have a good success rate, although it is certainly nowhere near 100%. Our method is based on learning theory and relies heavily on the concept of prompting very small behaviors and providing nearly immediate social and tangible reinforcers. The process is time consuming and requires patience and dedication on the part of the behavior analyst and the parents as well, but there can be a huge payoff—children under the age of 5 who receive at least 2 years of intensive one-on-one instruction often are able to function in a normal educational environment. It is important to note that this behaviorally based treatment for autism should be carried out in a very precise way by a qualified professional such as a Board Certified Behavior Analyst to assure any kind of success.[8]

> **"This study showed that with intensive one-on-one behavioral treatment (25–40 hours per week) about half of the children in the study appeared to actually recover from autism."**

---

[8]For more information on becoming a Board Certified Behavior Analyst, please see Chapter 8.

The follow-up on Catherine Maurice's children is certainly encouraging to anyone who finds that his or her young child has been diagnosed with autism; both of her children made full recoveries as a result of intensive behavioral treatment and were described by later teachers, who did not know of their initial diagnosis, as "academically advanced and socially well-adjusted." (Green, 1996).

● ●

Key Concepts:
Autism, behaviorally based treatment, certified behavior analyst

EXERCISE:

1. If you have an interest in the treatment of autistic children and want to learn more first hand, you could contact your local school system and ask to speak to someone about behaviorally based treatment of autism offered by the local school board. In the event that your local school system does not use or have access to behavioral services, another option would be to talk to a professional in your area about behaviorally based treatment. To find a behavior analyst to interview, go to the www.bacb.com Web site and search for a certified behavior analyst in your area. You might also want to check out some of the references that we have listed at the end of this book.

QUESTION #13.

We know that you can use behavior analysis with children, but what about with senior citizens or older people?

The principles of behavior as we understand them can be applied with people of any age—and senior citizens are no exception. For older people living at home, contingencies of reinforcement can be used to help to keep them motivated to do some very basic activities like eating properly and exercising. B.F. Skinner actually wrote a book precisely for this group called *Enjoy Old Age: A Practical Guide* (Skinner & Vaughan, 1983). In this extremely practical and helpful book, suggestions are provided for keeping in touch with the world, improving memory, thinking clearly, keeping busy, and getting along with people. Although there is not a great deal of research in this field, it will clearly become more important in the future when the millions of baby-boomers retire, especially for those who will eventually end up in a nursing home or assisted living facility. Even now we hear reports that nursing home operators are resorting to drugs and restraints to deal with behavior problems in their facilities. They clearly should consider hiring behavior analysts to help them prevent their residents from becoming dependent on staff for things they can do for themselves and to encourage their active participation in daily activities that will keep them alert and vigorous. We know the intelligent use of *environmental design* and more effective prompts can keep aging individuals in touch with their daily

B. F. Skinner

schedules as well as help them remember their grandchildren's names. We also know as people become older their reinforcers may change. Anyone who is charged with the care of people who are elderly will need to know how to do a *reinforcer survey* and how to use those reinforcers to motivate geriatric patients to ambulate on their own, take their medications, and learn leisure skills that will help them maintain their fine-motor coordination. An excellent book describing the behavioral approach to treating this population is *Behavior Analysis and Therapy in Nursing Homes* (Lundervold & Lewin, 1992).

• •

Key Concepts:
Environmental design, reinforcer survey

EXERCISE:

1. Find a local nursing home or senior center in your phone book and call to ask if you can interview someone there about behavior problems the staff might have with their residents. Make a list of the problems mentioned and then, using the *Journal of Applied Behavior Analysis* search engine, see if you can find any research that has been done on these problem areas.

QUESTION #14.
What do behavior analysts think about changing behavior in a business setting?

The application of behavior analysis in business settings is referred to as *performance management* (Daniels & Daniels, 2004). This area has been around since the early 1970s and is currently a vigorous and active area of consulting practice and applied research. The basic principles of behavior that work in homes and schools and rehabilitation facilities work in business and industry as well, with the additional benefit that changes in behavior can have an economic payoff. Applied research has been conducted in a wide variety of settings, from small, family-owned businesses to Fortune 500 corporate giants. The range of problems that have been tackled includes improving warehouse dock sorting and loading procedures to improving leadership in the boardroom. In our increasingly service-oriented economy, improving customer service is essential for restaurants, hotels, and retail chains to remain competitive, and here there has evolved a very clear strategy for managers to employ. Rather than assuming that every performance problem requires more training, a behavior analyst will think, "I wonder why the service is so poor here? I know they've all been through training, but they still don't attend to customers, don't offer to answer questions, and don't do any follow up."

Thinking like a behavior analyst yields questions about whether the performance that is desired has been prompted, whether the supervisor gives any feedback or praise when the behavior does occur, and whether there is some competing behavior actually being reinforced (e.g., talking on the phone when the sales associate should be waiting on customers). A behavior analyst consulting with a business will start by asking diagnostic questions like these and then determine which to address depending on the answers and baseline data that are collected for the business. Working directly with management, a performance improvement plan will be drawn up that is custom designed for that setting and then implemented over days or weeks and evaluated online to determine if it is effective in achieving preestablished goals and objectives. In business and industry it is important to focus on both the performance of the employees and the results of their behavior. Other approaches to improving business practice often stress only the results and are likely to fail because they don't treat the underlying behavior that produces the results.

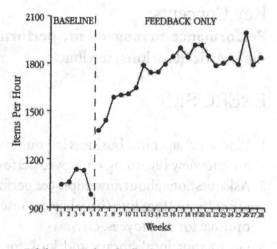

Exhibit 6.   When feedback was given to key-punch operators in a bank, performance related to proofing checks and deposits nearly doubled.

An early study in performance management illustrates the power of a fairly simple change of procedures. At the Union National Bank, the managers were interested in increasing the proofing of checks and deposits of their keypunch operators. They had been trained well, but the consultant working with the bank discovered they rarely, if ever, got any feedback on their performance. As can be seen in this graph, simply by providing feedback on their performance (a form of immediate reinforcement) they were able to nearly double the performance.

Key Concepts:
Performance management, performance improvement plan, diagnostic questions, feedback

EXERCISES:

1. Find a manager in a business in your town and ask if you may conduct an interview regarding employee performance.
2. Ask questions about any employee performance problems that seem to affect the bottom line (i.e., they cut into profits, increase costs, are not optimal for employees, etc.).
3. Go to your local library and look for the *Journal of Organizational Behavior Management* and look for any articles that address any problems that resemble the ones you learned about in your interview.
4. Prepare a mock performance improvement plan based on your reading of *Journal of Organizational Behavior Management* and the text by Daniels and Daniels (2004).

QUESTION #15.

What about other areas of application such as the community? Does behavior analysis work there too?

Behavior analysts have been busy working in a wide variety of settings over the past 40 years. In addition to well known applications of behavior analysis such as working with people with developmental disabilities or in classrooms with disruptive children, behavior analysts have been thinking of ways to improve other aspects of our culture as well.

Behavioral community psychology is the application of behavioral principles and procedures to community-wide problems. Behavior analysts have made significant contributions to finding effective solutions for addressing community problems as diverse as getting citizens to save gas by forming car pools; saving energy by getting homeowners to lower their thermostats, reducing litter in public settings; and increasing the recycling of paper, cans, and glass.

Each of these applications addresses problems that are faced on a large scale by communities everywhere. The benefits that result from the use of behavioral technology to solve community problems include saving substantial amounts of money as well as improving and protecting the environment for future generations.

Another area in which behavior analysis has played an important role is in the area of animal training (see the Cambridge Center for Behavioral Studies at www.behavior.org). There are more than 60 million pet dogs and 70 million pet cats in the United States. Each year, in animals shelters across the country, nearly 14 million animals are euthanized, many because of behavior problems (that are easily treatable). Excessive barking, jumping on company, snapping at children, and urinating on the new white carpet are behaviors that earn many animals a one-way ticket to an overcrowded animal shelter that will ultimately have no choice but to euthanize the animal.

Behavior analysts are making a difference by making animal training technologies and behavioral assistance available to the general public. Owners can attend classes at dog clubs, go to seminars, or attend class at a local pet superstore.

Also in the animal world, behavior analysts are involved in improving the lives of animals in settings from a to z, aquariums to zoos. Elephants are trained to raise their feet to receive routine foot care that can save their lives. Dolphins are trained to swim into a net to receive medical assessments and care, and in most settings that have captive animals, behaviorally based enrichment programs are now in place.

From infants to geriatrics, work behaviors, employees, at home, in the community, every kind of disability, animal training, pets, nonpet animals, specialized skills such as sports and flying jet planes, health and exercise, getting along with others, improving relationships ... if it involves behavior, behavior analysts can help.

•••

Key Concepts:
Behavioral community psychology, animal training

EXERCISES:

1. Describe a behavior problem in your community (e.g., litter at the playground). Assuming city officials gave you the resources needed, describe a behavior plan to fix this.
2. You've either grown up with pets or seen the pets of neighbors or relatives. What are some of the pet behavior problems you've seen or know about? Describe one animal behavior problem and give a description of a behavior plan to address the problem.
3. Take a look at the Animal Behavior section of the Cambridge Center for Behavioral Studies (www.behavior.org). Briefly list several applications of behavior analysis with animals.

QUESTION #16.

What do you think the future holds for behavior analysis research? Is it primarily focusing on developmentally disabled individuals?

Far from it! Just in the past few years, we have seen breakthrough research conducted in a number of new and exciting areas of application. Behavior analysts are working with college students on improving generalized use of computer-interactive mathematics (Ninness et al., 2005), enhanced quiz performance (Ryan & Hemmes, 2005), and teaching abduction-prevention skills to young children (Johnson et al., 2005). Other new research involves working with restaurant owners to increase the greeting of customers (Therrien, Wilder, Rodriguez, & Wine, 2005) and the completion of closing tasks (Austin, Weatherly, & Gravina, 2005) and working with traffic engineers to increase seatbelt use with motorists (Van Houten, Malenfant, Austin, & Lebbon, 2005) and to reduce vehicle conflicts at traffic exits (Van Houten, Malenfant, Zhao, Ko, & Van Houten, 2005).

Some very stimulating work is going on in behavioral economics (Roane, Call, & Falcomata, 2005) and health and safety. In the health and safety areas, behavioral researchers have studied internet-based methods of maintaining smoking abstinence (Dallery & Glenn, 2005) as well as methods of modifying cigarette smoking by adolescents (Roll, 2005) and teaching effective gun safety to children (Miltenberger et al., 2005).

Clearly, the way is now wide open for behavior analysts to take on almost any pressing problem in our culture, from large-scale issues like seat-belt use and traffic safety to business applications and theories of behavioral economics. Behavior analysts continue to have a great interest in working with developmentally disabled and autistic children, but their work with normal children and the modern challenges of living in a complex world of guns and predators has not escaped their notice or interest.

We expect this groundbreaking research to continue well into the future, with behavior analysts tackling some of the most important behaviorally relevant problems of our time, including big issues such as developing effective leaders (Daniels & Daniels, 2005), finding the most effective way to pay for work performance (Abernathy, 1996), and learning how to design environments for optimal behavioral safety (Geller, 2001).

● ●

Key Concepts:
Current *Journal of Applied Behavior Analysis* **research, future of behavior analysis**

EXERCISE:

1. Look in your local newspaper for articles that have to do with human behavior that you find interesting. Go to the *Journal of Applied Behavior Analysis* Web site and type in keywords related to this type of behavior and see if you can find any research on this topic.

Three

The Science and
Technology of Behavior

QUESTION #17.

Behavioral research methods seem to be quite different from any other psychology that I have studied, is that right?

If you're asking questions about research methods, there's a good chance you're a student who has taken psychology classes in which you've learned about research that is based on statistics. If you've come to the conclusion that behavioral research methods are different from those used in statistical research, you are 100% correct.

Although the methods that behavior analysts use in their research are very common to scientists in biology, medicine, chemistry, and other related fields, they are not really like those used in the rest of psychology. We owe our origins to primarily to B.F. Skinner (1938, 1953), who established the framework for the field with his early laboratory work and subsequently inspired several generations of applied researchers to work with populations who could benefit from a technology of human behavior. Skinner essentially taught us to think like behavior analysts when we look at what a person does or says.

In Skinner's early work he showed that fundamental principles of behavior could be found by studying a small number of "subjects" over a long period of time. Although Skinner worked primarily with rats and pigeons, researchers who came after him found that this same general approach also worked well with human participants. In fact, as it turns out, most of the important variables that are

> **"In Skinner's early work, he showed that fundamental principles of behavior could be found by studying a small number of "subjects" over a long period of time."**

relevant for individuals really have to be studied in this way to determine effective treatments; findings from group statistical research often have very little relevance for individuals in need of treatment, whereas within-subject research is ideally suited to individual cases such as those involving managed care (Morgan & Morgan, 2001).

Statistical research began in agriculture where researchers wanted to know the effects of seasonal crop rotations or adding certain kinds of fertilizers to their fields. Statistics is relevant for an application like this because the "statistically significant" effects would accumulate over the many thousands of acres that might be studied, but when we are looking at humans and trying to change behavior, it is important that we have a clear picture of how each individual is performing. There's an old joke that goes like this. "What is a statistician?" Answer: "It's a person who with his head in an oven and his feet in a freezer says, 'Well, on the average, I feel fine.'" In behavior analysis research, we rely on the technology for research started by Skinner to help us look carefully at individual performance. Using statistics for what we do would yield results comparable to mixing many colors of paint and ending up with a color that looks like none of the originals. For example, if you are going to observe disruptive children in a classroom, you could take data on the number of times the children acted out. Using a statistical research model, you would most likely average those numbers together. This could create a false impression, because the child you need to target is the one who is getting out of his seat 34 times, not all of the children, whose disruptions average 4 per day. For this reason, we use the research methodology of behavior analysis called *single-subject design*. Behavior analysts who studied this classroom of disruptive children would evaluate each child's data independently of the other children's.

As Skinner developed a science of individual behavior, he had to first learn how to quantify individual performance over time—and for this he needed an apparatus. He discovered if he created a small working environment where his pigeons and rats could operate a mechanism and receive food reinforcers, he could determine a great deal about their behavior. This apparatus was an *operant chamber* and became known as a "Skinner box." Skinner found he could shape animals to press a lever or peck a key under some conditions and not others (green key vs. red key) or to work at a fast and furious rate or very slowly and he could teach a very complex skill that involved a chain of behaviors that were shaped independently and then linked together. His findings were replicated by other behavioral researchers at other universities and ultimately were extended to many species, including, of course, humans.

In Skinner's system, each individual subject or participant essentially serves as his or her own control, thus eliminating the need for a control group. The science of behavior that Skinner espoused consists of thousands and thousands of studies performed over half a century that clearly show that certain important variables consistently affect human performance.

We can use behavior analysis research methods to study the behavior of individual people in one setting or across settings, we can look at performance during both treatment and no-treatment conditions, and we can look at groups such as one classroom compared to another using single-subject research design.

In short, the research methods used in applied behavior analysis have evolved to the point that applied behavioral researchers can study everyday human behavior in almost any setting[9] (Bailey & Burch, 2002).

● ●

Key Concepts:
Behavior analytic research, single-subject design

EXERCISES:

1. If we were working with 25 adults in a sheltered workshop, why would we not want to use statistics to evaluate increases in the length of time they were on task? Basically, how would you evaluate improvements in performance (on-task behavior) in this setting?
2. Read a study in which statistics are used to quantify the results. What can you determine about the performance of individual participants from these results?

---

[9]Laboratory research in operant conditioning still continues and is published primarily in *The Journal of the Experimental Analysis of Behavior* and applied work with humans is published in *The Journal of Applied Behavior Analysis* and about a dozen other applied journals (for listing, please see Appendix).

QUESTION #18.
What is the difference between behavioral *research* and behavioral *treatment?*

You may have noticed that behavior analysts take data both when they are treating a client and when they are conducting research. In many respects *behavior treatment* looks a lot like the *behavioral research* from which it is derived. Both clinicians and researchers take baseline data, implement interventions, and provide ongoing evaluations of the interventions.

However, researchers have to use well accepted and thoroughly tested protocols for their research. As an example of one requirement of good research, behavioral researchers must perform interobserver reliability (IOR) checks, whereas clinicians usually do not carry out such checks. So, if a behavior analyst was providing behavioral treatment for a child, she might observe that child, take daily data, and report the results to the habilitation team. If this were research, she would have to adhere to

research standards. Most likely, the behavior analyst would not be taking the data on the treatment that she provided because she might be accused of being biased. She would have to have more than one observer watching the child and taking data. These two people would not talk to each other as they observe and record the data. At the end of the session, the researcher, would calculate IOR, which is a measure of agreement between the two observers. If needed, the researcher would give additional training to the observers.

Although this level of experimental rigor is not required during behavioral treatment, you should adhere to as many of the standards for research as possible.

Researchers must also strive to test for social validation of their methods. *Social validation* answers questions about whether or not consumers or the public would find this research useful. Behavioral therapists rarely have to test for social validation. The fact that consumers want behavioral services provides the social validation that is needed.

Many behavioral consultants working in large organizations routinely use research protocols in their practices to demonstrate to corporate customers the results they are achieving are valid and reliable. To clearly show systematic changes in behavior, they will employ sophisticated research designs demonstrating that intervention effects were due to certain specific inputs and precise measurement of outcomes.

● ●

Key Concepts:
Behavioral research, behavioral treatment, research protocol, social validation

EXERCISES:

1. What are some of the extra requirements of behavioral research?
2. Observe a client-training program in a facility or school. Assuming that the necessary approvals could be obtained, would it be possible to make this training program into a research project? What research questions might you ask?

QUESTION #19.

Is it really possible to find the cause of a certain behavior?

Behavior analysts are practical, reasonable people who are fascinated by human behavior. They are nearly obsessed with two questions: First, why did this behavior occur—what caused it? And second, what can I do to improve this behavior for this person, that is, how can I help her have a higher-quality life, with less pain and frustration and more enjoyment? Before we can begin to approach the second question we must first answer the "Why?" question.

Being practical people, when behavior analysts ask the Why question, we are not talking about the original cause of the behavior. Instead, we are talking about what is going on right now that is prompting or maintaining the responses we can see

"Behavior analysts are practical, reasonable people who are fascinated by human behavior."

that are making the person miserable or causing those around the person to suffer. To find the answer to this question, we use a procedure developed in 1982 by Brian Iwata and his colleagues.[10] The procedure is called *experimental functional analysis* or *functional analysis* for short. Simply put, we believe that a behavior that is occurring with some regularity is producing some effect that is maintaining it.

Jason is a 9-year-old who is having problems in his elementary school classroom. Jason's frustrated teacher has referred him for behavioral services because he spends so much time off task and being disruptive. Jason daydreams at his desk, and when he is really fired up, he will climb on the desk and try to make the other students laugh. Jason was referred to the

---

[10]This work was done at The John F. Kennedy Institute and Johns Hopkins University School of Medicine.

school behavior analyst. Before observing or conducting any assessments, she wondered if Jason's off-task and disruptive behaviors are occurring because (a) the material is too difficult and he is trying to avoid the work, (b) it is very reinforcing to make noises and make the other children laugh, or (c) because when he is off task or disruptive, the teacher comes around and talks to him, giving him encouragement and prompting to get back on task. The experienced school behavior analyst is not certain what the problem is, but she is convinced it is either one of these three possibilities or some other variable she hasn't identified just yet.

At this point in addressing Jason's behavior problem, as behavior analysts, we would do a functional analysis in which we would carefully evaluate each of these variables one at a time to determine what happens to the behavior. If we think math problems are too difficult for Jason, we'd give him some easier problems on certain days to determine if there is any effect on disruptive, off-task behavior. On other days he would have his regular math worksheet, but we would cue the teacher to attend to him only when he is on task, and so on. Through this process of systematically trying one variable after another and then repeating each variable, we can isolate the cause of Jason's off-task and disruptive behavior, and we can use this information to find the very best intervention for him.

If the behavior analyst does not have the time or resources to do a full-blown functional analysis, she may decide that she will conduct a *functional assessment* instead. This involves nonexperimental methods such as informal observation, interviewing key personnel and asking diagnostic questions, or conducting rather formal direct observations using a systematic method of data collection. The purpose of all of these functional assessment procedures is to help the behavior analyst locate some variable that looks like it might be the controlling variable. Then, once a variable is targeted, there is some trial period during which a treatment plan is implemented on a pilot basis to see if the guess was right. The behavior analyst working in the classroom with Jason may interview the teacher and ask, "What happens when Jason is off task? Does it seem to happen only during certain class periods? If so, what subject matter is he working on?" These and other related questions might lead the behavior analyst to hypothesize that, "Jason's off-task and disruptive behavior, from all reports, seems to occur just during math and geography classes. I'm thinking that maybe those are two difficult subjects for him. Let's try him on some easier material for a few days and see what happens." During this pilot phase data will be collected and the behavior analyst should know in a short period whether her hypothesis is right or not. If it is, the behavior analyst will write up a behavior program that will be given to the teacher to implement. Jason's parents will also be informed of the behavior program, asked to sign consent forms, and given an opportunity to ask questions about the plan for addressing Jason's behavioral issues.

• •

Key Concepts:
Cause of behavior, functional analysis, functional assessment, behavior program

EXERCISES:

1. Louis is a 12-year-old boy with severe mental retardation. When he is sitting in his wheelchair, he will rub his eyes with the palm of his hand. His eyes get very red and irritated from this. Why is it important to know the cause of this behavior before treating it?
2. If you were asked to conduct a functional analysis on the eye rubbing behavior, what are some questions you might ask?
3. Suppose the functional assessment showed that Louis engaged in eye rubbing for attention. What are some procedures you might use in a behavior program to treat eye rubbing?

QUESTION #20.

I took my dog to obedience school and he learned to walk on a leash, sit, and stay, but he still jumps on people at home and he won't come when I call him if he gets loose in the neighborhood. Does this mean that behavior shaping doesn't work with dogs?

From where we sit as behavior analysts, we have to say right off the bat that behavior is behavior, regardless of the organism: canine or coach, feline or florist, it doesn't matter from our perspective; the principles always apply.

One thing we know for sure is that animal behavior has been thoroughly explored by many different professionals. For decades animal behavior has been the subject of study from many different perspectives, including experimental psychology, ethology, veterinary medicine, animal trainers, use in police and military K-9 units, and behavior analysis (Burch & Bailey, 1999).

It's amazing to us how so many people trained in behavior analysis have so little knowledge when it comes to training or managing the behavior of their own pets. Related to the dog question previous, one of the first things every responsible dog owner should do after finding a veterinarian is to locate an obedience

> **"From where we sit as behavior analysts, we have to say right off the bat that behavior is behavior, regardless of the organism."**

school. This pertains even to behavior analysts, who may think they know all they need to know about training a dog. Dogs are a different species from children with autism, so you will need some species-specific training. When your dog is a puppy, you should begin training in the basics of sit, stay, down, come, and walking on a leash. Generally you will enroll for a 6 to 8 week class that meets once per week. Each week you will learn how to train a new behavior and will be given homework exercises. The purpose of the homework is not only to reinforce the new behaviors, but also to *train for generalization* to your home setting and neighborhood.

This generalization from your obedience school in a local recreational center or gym can often be difficult and probably will not be automatic. You should expect that you will have to practice the skills you learned at obedience school over and over at home until your pup can sit, stay, down, come, and walk on a leash just as nicely at home as the dog does with your instructor present. You should not expect that because your dog can sit at school that the animal will generalize this to a down at home—it doesn't work that way unless you train for generalization.

In the situation described in the question, the problem was not that "behavior shaping doesn't work." The problem was that the skills did not generalize to other settings. You need to practice what you learn at the obedience training class at home in your living room, in your yard, and in the community. For jumping on people who come into the house, teach an alternate behavior such as sit–stay or down–stay. For not coming when called if your dog gets loose, first, invest in a better fence and teach family members to close the door. This may sound sarcastic, but remember, a part of managing behavior is analyzing the environment.

Then, start with calling your dog from short distances and provide a tasty treat when your dog comes to you.

● ●

Key Concepts:
Generalization, training for generalization

EXERCISES:

1. In everyday life, the failure of skills to generalize happens frequently with motor skills. People often have a hard time adjusting to novel golf courses, tennis courts, and computer equipment or from their home piano to the one at the piano teacher's house. ("I swear, I practiced 2 hours every day!") Think about something you might have learned or been taught in the past. Were there any problems with the generalization of your newly acquired skills?
2. If you teach a client with developmental disabilities how to do a specific leisure skill at a day-training program, what should you do to ensure the client uses the skill at home?

Chapter

Four

General Issues
of Behavior

QUESTION #21.
Does behavior analysis work with groups?

Although behavior analysts most often think in terms of individual behavior, we also are interested in what happens with behavior that is seen in groups. Small groups such as teams in business or sports are often the focus of behavior analysts who may be called in to improve performance. From our perspective, the difference between individual and group behavior is the members of the group may get involved in prompting behavior and applying contingencies to each other. Sometimes people choose to participate in groups, such as when they have joined a softball team and want to compete. Natural reinforcers such as winning a league trophy require that the individual members of the team respond to each other in cooperative and supportive ways. Although cooperation may not necessarily benefit an individual team member, it results in a team accomplishment. This is known as a *group contingency*, and it can produce both good and bad behavior within the group. As an example of bad behavior resulting from a group contingency, individual members of the team might size up other players and conclude they are not highly motivated, and then engage in coercive tactics to produce a more energetic performance out of them. On a positive note, members of a team might become very encouraging and supportive; they could provide a new form of reinforcement, called *social reinforcement*, which is not available when a person is operating individually. When behavior analysts are called in to improve the performance of a team—whether in sports or in a business setting—they look for consequences that can be added or enhanced. They may even train the individual members of the team in how to prompt and reinforce other team members, thus adding a subtle form of influence that would not exist otherwise.

Group contingencies are also present in business settings. Take, for example, a business that provides technical assistance on computer software

problems via phone and e-mail. In such companies, associates sit in cubicles and take calls and e-mails individually, although they are considered a "technical assistance group" by their manager. Some of the associates may eagerly answer as many calls as possible, whereas others may slack off and do much less work.

As is often the case, all of the members of this group are paid the same biweekly salary, regardless of individual performance. A performance management consultant may recommend a new group contingency designed to encourage associates to persuade their teammates to work a little harder, taking more calls and completing them more quickly. "If your group can achieve an average of 95% of completed calls in less than 5 minutes each, everyone gets a bonus; if not, no one gets a bonus." As you might imagine, individual team members, especially those very interested in the bonus, might do a little cheerleading to keep their colleagues pumped up and possibly discourage some off-task behavior: "Isn't it time we got back to the phones? Our coffee break is up and we are very close to earning that bonus!"

The first author has consulted on many performance management projects with small businesses over the past 20 years and has seen owners and managers demonstrate their complete lack of understanding of the use of reinforcement with groups: it's called "Employee of the Month." In a typical scheme, the owner announces somewhat grandly that at the end of the month one employee who "is truly outstanding" will be selected as the winner. The person's name will be put on a plaque by the front entrance and the lucky winner will be able to park in a special reserved parking space. What this well meaning owner doesn't realize is a system like this basically produces only one winner and a whole lot of losers. When an Employee of the Month program goes bad, some of the losers will be disgruntled and possibly angry they didn't get selected. They might talk behind the supervisor's back about how this is unfair and shows favoritism. In some cases, employees who did not win will talk to people in the office about how the winner is a slacker who gets a lot of help with his or her work. The next thing you know, not only will employees who didn't win not be motivated, but quite the opposite; they might develop a serious morale problem.

There may be isolated cases where Employee of the Month programs are liked and enjoyed by many of the employees. In some settings, any festive activity to break up the monotonous routine of the office is welcomed. However, supervisors should realize that although these programs

> **"A business owner or supervisor wanting to motivate a group of employees needs to understand the downside of competition in the workplace."**

may bring fun and employee recognition to the workplace, there is no demonstrated link to improved productivity or performance.

A business owner or supervisor wanting to motivate a group of employees needs to understand the downside of competition in the workplace and consider other options that will directly reinforce each and every employee who tries harder to meet company goals. A small bonus for everyone who meets some criterion, individually set to be fair, is a much better option, for example.

Applying the basic principles of behavior in any group can be a tricky business and we usually recommend that anyone considering this option consult with a Board Certified Behavior Analyst before proceeding.

Key Concepts:
Group contingency

EXERCISES:

1. Visit a restaurant or coffee shop and observe the behavior of the wait staff, staff who bus tables, and hosts or hostesses. Identify examples of teamwork, as opposed to individual performance.
2. Count the number of team behaviors that involve helping one another, as well as missed opportunities for such cooperative behavior.
3. If you are a sports fan, observe a basketball, baseball, soccer, or football game. Identify the team behaviors that make one team more successful than another.
4. Look on the *Journal of Applied Behavior Analysis* Web site (http//: seab.envmed.rochester.edu/jaba/) and search for articles on sports or team sports.

QUESTION #22.
What is a history of reinforcement? Do people have their own unique histories of reinforcement?

A history of reinforcement is a concept that describes what happens to you as you have various experiences day after day, year after year. In some cases, people have a one-time exposure to a contingency that changes the way in which they behave long-term.

Sara and Susie are identical twins. Their mother dresses them in identical dresses and puts the same color ribbons in their curly blond hair. They have always attended the same schools, they've had the same teachers, and they have come into contact with the same kinds of reinforcers for similar behaviors .

On a beautiful spring day when the twins were 3 years old, Susie was playing in the back yard and picked up a stick that turned out to be a snake. The small poisonous snake bit her on the arm. Mom heard Susie crying and raced out into the yard, grabbed her up, and rushed her to the emergency room. Luckily, this emergency room had the snake antivenin that was needed to prevent Susie from losing her arm.

Fast-forward 3 years. The twins are now 6 years old. Susie recovered nicely, but she developed a dislike for playing outside and she spends her time indoors reading books, drawing pictures, and watching television. Sara, Susie's identical twin, continued play outside, developing her gross motor skills and getting to know the children who lived next door.

It doesn't take too much imagination to conceive of the snake-bite incident as the beginning of a major difference in the history of reinforcement for these two little girls. Beginning with that one incident, Susie was reinforced for staying inside and she developed somewhat of a phobia about being outdoors alone. Sara never had the experience with the snake. She grew up wanting to play outside and loving nature. As a teenager, she took up sports, and she is starting a career in wildlife management. Susie developed normally, and even though it meant a lot of time being separated from her twin, she never did develop any interest in being outside. She became an English professor who wrote short stories and poems. Her job requires that she spend a great deal of time in the library and on the computer.

Each day you engage in behaviors that bring certain kinds of consequences. These consequences shape your overall repertoire and increase the likelihood you will engage in certain behaviors and find others less and less reinforcing. Over time, your repertoire will become fairly fixed. Based on years of working closely with college students, parents, and employees in professional settings, our observations suggest that this seems to happen by about age 25 or so. At this point, you have a long history of reinforcement that guides your day-to-day behavior with an invisible hand. This history of reinforcement predicts what you will like, what you will do, and what choices you will make. When you meet someone new who you find interesting, you are looking at a person who has been shaped by experiences and a whole series of reinforcement contingencies. It is these contingencies that make people unique.

"This history of reinforcement predicts what you will like, what you will do, and what choices you will make."

If you want to understand a person you are getting to know, you will need to ask questions about the person's history of reinforcement. "How did you get interested in skydiving anyway?" It is unlikely the person will have a good understanding of exactly how this happened, so their description will probably be incomplete. "Oh, I don't know. One day my roommate said, 'Hey, I'm going skydiving. Do you want to ride along and watch?'" If this person isn't a behavior analyst, he or she will leave out the history of reinforcement that led up to this adventuresome spirit, but a listener who has good behavior analysis skills will figure it out.

A person's history of reinforcement is invisible to the rest of the world. It doesn't leave any scars, but you can see some clues if you study a person carefully for a period of time. You can deduce a history of reinforcement from how people respond to certain situations. What people order in restaurants, how they eat, and what they talk about over dinner provides plenty of clues about a person's history of reinforcement. Some people have food aversions that are no doubt a result of a bad experience such as food poisoning, or they have strong preferences for certain drinks, preferring only bottled water or a certain type of hard-to-find beer. You can also gain an understanding about a close friend's relationship with her loser boyfriend:

> **"A person's history of reinforcement is invisible to the rest of "**

> "So why do you keep going back to him? He yells at you and pushes you around. ..." "You don't really see him like I do, he's really sweet; sometimes he likes to cuddle. I think he really adores me, it's just that sometimes he's having a bad day down at the shop and I guess I get in his way. It's all my fault, really. ..."

The basic message a behavior analyst would read from this exchange is that your friend is on an intermittent schedule of reinforcement. Sometimes the boyfriend delivers wonderful, touching reinforcers and sometimes he delivers angry, mean-spirited punishers. Your friend is telling you that, all things considered, the reinforcers are more powerful (although she is most likely unaware it is due to the power of the intermittent schedule of reinforcement).

The first author has a personal history of reinforcement story in the form of overdosing on strawberries when he was a child. On a fine summer day in northwestern Pennsylvania, he went to pick strawberries with his grandmother. It was one of those perfect days, with big puffy clouds and a temperature about 80°. The farmer gave them baskets and said, "I charge by the basket. Have fun." Jon started down the rows looking for juicy ripe berries to take home. He was already thinking of the strawberry jam his grandmother would make that weekend. They would also have strawberry shortcake with delicious warm, homemade biscuits that only she could make, and there would be fresh homemade whipped cream on top. But it was 80°, he was working hard, and he started to get parched. "I could have one of those juicy strawberries right now just to see how they taste …," and so he did.

It was delicious, and so was the next one and the one after that. You can guess what happened. Soon, Jon was eating one strawberry for each one dropped in the basket. On the long drive home, he began to feel a little nauseated and he crawled into the back seat. The 1954 Dodge sedan tossed and turned down the winding road. Fortunately, his grandmother had quick reflexes and was able to pull over to the side of the road just in time for Jon to lunge out of back seat onto the side of the road where he spewed a torrent of bright red, semidigested liquid into the bushes.

Some people never recover from an experience like this and they swear off the offending food item forever. In Jon's case, about 10 years later, he was able to eat strawberries again. Nonetheless, this is just exactly how a history of reinforcement works. Other experiences produce different effects and also contribute to lifelong preferences. A 5-year-old rides out to the private airport with his dad to watch the small aircraft take off. They are able to get close enough they can feel the propwash streaming off of a two-seater Cessna as it makes a turn onto the runway, and the noise of the engine revving is palpable. It seems like magic to watch the plane glide down the runway and dip its wings just before it disappears into the clear blue. This sort of intensive, one-time experience can make little boy want to fly and might control his choices for many years. Or, a mother saves her money at Christmastime to take her 6-year-old daughter to see *The Nutcracker* ballet. Somewhere between "The Dance of the Flowers" and the appearance of the Sugarplum Fairy, the little girl decides she wants to be a dancer. A lot of other things have to happen for this to occur, but the initial pairing has taken place.

One final example is a little frightening in its implications. A teenager stops at the Quick Stop convenience store on the way home from school, drops some change in the Coke® machine and, gets … nothing. He has no more change and feels like he's been ripped off. He gives the machine a flat-handed, stiff-armed shove and suddenly, that familiar clunk-clunk comes from the flap in the machine. Out comes his Coke and then another one, and he gets his change back! Knowing what we know about history of reinforcement, the behavior analyst would observe that hitting, shoving, and punching have just been reinforced, and quite immediately, at that. We would predict under similar circumstances this behavior will occur again; and we might worry about the possibility of generalization from vending machines to people. All this young man needs is a couple of instances when he pushes someone and gets his way to set in motion a chain of events that could easily lead to a whole repertoire of threatening and aggressive behaviors that are reinforced on an intermittent basis. Fast-forward to college. Now this young man has met a girl, he dates her a few times, then starts pushing for intimacy that she resists. He raises his voice, threatens, and she gives in. Now he has been reinforced once more for the same behavior that started so long ago with a malfunctioning vending machine. This is how a history of reinforcement is developed and how it can play out over time. It pays to be aware of contingencies of reinforcement and to understand the powerful effect they can have on behavior once they become part of a person's history of reinforcement.

It may seem like a stretch to go from a young man kicking a soft-drink machine to abusing a woman several years later. But, as hard to believe as it may seem, reinforcement can work like this. Serial killers don't go from being model citizens one day to murdering people the next. Most of these documented cases show a history that includes picking on other children, then progressing to hurting them, then engaging in animal abuse and more.

Understanding a person's history of reinforcement is critical to understanding the person's behavior.

> " Understanding a person's history of reinforcement is critical to understanding the person's behavior. "

•••

Key Concepts:
History of reinforcement, contingencies of reinforcement

EXERCISES:

1. Explain what we mean by history of reinforcement.
2. A college student who had poor judgment had something big to celebrate, so he went out with his friends and drank an excessive amount of alcoholic beverages. He woke up violently ill and spent the better part of the night hugging the toilet bowl. When he was able to call his friends a few days later, he said would never touch tequila again. How do you explain in behavioral terms what happened here?
3. How can you explain the behavior of gang members who are young people who steal and will commit murder to protect the gang?
4. Cathy likes to visit her friend who lives in a big city. The friend has a roommate who wants to pal around and be a part of all the activities. The problem is, every time they are somewhere having fun, the roommate says she does not feel well and that she wants everyone to stop what they are doing, get in a cab, and take her home. She really doesn't appear to be sick. Explain how the roommate's behavior ("I'm sick, let's all go home") might have developed.

QUESTION #23.

Is all behavior learned?

Holding hands as they walked out of a darkened matinee movie theater one bright summer afternoon, an older couple seemed to be enjoying themselves, until the man started sneezing. These were ultraloud, supersonic sneezes, the kind that made people who were nearby turn and stare. "Why do you have to be so darn loud?" said the embarrassed wife. Between sneezes, the man snapped, "I can't help it! I'm not doing it on purpose."

So, what do you think about Sneezy? Is he guilty? Maybe. Maybe not. Some people sneeze and use their voices to scream a loud, "AH-CHOO!" The yelling along with the sneeze is operant or learned behavior. But, the actual sneeze can't be helped. Bright sunlight can actually elicit sneezing. Sneezing is in a  category called respondent behavior. Respondent behavior is a form of behavior that is not "learned" in the same sense as operant behaviors. Respondent behaviors can be conditioned and they involve reflexes. In our daily lives we engage in respondent behaviors and operant behaviors. Our guess is the ratio of the first to the second is probably 1:20. Each day, almost everything we do that is important to us is learned or operant behavior. The remainder of behaviors are respondent and they are so unusual they really do stand out when they occur. As behavior analysts, we are almost entirely interested in learned or operant behaviors; we have some interest in respondent behaviors, especially if they are contributing some misery to a person's life. Some very important emotions and troublesome behaviors fit into the category of conditioned respondent behavior. A child is bitten by a dog and develops a fear or phobia of dogs. This is respondent conditioning at work, and the treatment for such behaviors requires a thorough understanding of respondent conditioning and the therapies associated with such behaviors. The field of behavior therapy is largely devoted to the treatment of anxieties, fears, phobias, and related traumatic behaviors most likely caused by some sort of respondent conditioning.

So, the short answer is not all behavior is learned; respondent behaviors—such as an eye blink in the presence of a sudden puff of air near the eye or sneezes that are the result of exposure to sunshine—are automatic. But for the most part, the important behaviors in people's lives are learned motor behaviors that are both large and small, simple and complex. You learn how to drive a car, memorize a PIN number, or give a speech; these are all learned behaviors.

• •

Key Concepts:
Respondent behaviors, operant behaviors, learned behaviors

EXERCISES:

1. What is a respondent behavior? Give an example.
2. Is all behavior learned? Why or why not?
3. What is an operant behavior? Give an example.

QUESTION #24.

Can you really replace a behavior?
Can habits really be broken?

As behavior analysts, we think of behaviors in terms of their function, that is, what consequence do they produce? And, as we have described before, those functions include things such as getting attention from others, escape from an aversive situation, acquisition of tangible goods, and so on. The list is long, and the consequences are unique from one person to the next. Some people will do almost anything to be left alone; others will go to any length to have the spotlight shine on them. In some cases the reinforcers controlling a behavior are intrinsic to the activity itself and require no intervention by anyone else. Solving crossword puzzles, reading, and gardening are all activities with such strong built-in consequences that involvement by others is irrelevant. In contrast, acting, dancing, playing sports, teaching, and consulting are

behaviors that are clearly maintained by the behavior of others.

When we look at any given behavior, our first thought as behavior analysts is, "Why are they doing that?" An elderly Southern woman dressed in her church clothes was sitting in the food court at the mall one Sunday afternoon. Her hair was teased in an old-fashioned beehive hairdo, she had on her shiny white shoes, and as she ate her lunch she looked around and began to stare. "Would you look at that!" she said to her daughter. "What in the world ...?!" She was looking at a group of teenagers who were dressed

all in black, including heavy boots and long coats, and, on closer inspection, who had pierced eyebrows and lips.

The tone of her voice suggested this very proper woman was basically disgusted by these youths and a rewording of her rhetorical question would be something like, "These kids are awful, horrible, and degrading; they should be removed from the mall immediately."

Behavior analysts would have an interesting perspective on these young people. One thing to think about is what consequences were maintaining such unusual behavior. The clothing must be uncomfortable. Look at the tall guy. The lug nut has put in a giant hole in his ear, along with the multiple piercings near his eyes, in his nose and lower lip, and in the center of his tongue, for cryin' out loud, had to be painful. Our guess is the reinforcers for such unusual behavior comes primarily from the peer group. There is possibly some accidental reinforcement from the parents, who make half-hearted attempts at disapproval, not realizing in their childrearing they have somehow made disapproval into a reinforcer. If the parents of these "mall rats" wanted to change their behavior, they should start by asking questions about the function of the unusual dress. Is it for attention? If so, perhaps a leisure activity could be found that would result in the young person gaining attention. Playing in a band or exhibiting original art pieces might meet the need for attention. Another option for parents who couldn't bear to take the approach of "this too shall pass" with regard to the unusual dress would be to specify times and places that counterculture clothes were okay. "You can wear this when you go out with your friends, but for Christmas dinner, going to church, and watching your dad get an award at the country club, please wear dress-up clothes."

Several years ago, the second author was consulting and teaching volunteers in an animal shelter how to train dogs. A 16-year-old girl who was sentenced to community service by the court system had been assigned to work at the shelter. Most of the problems that landed her in court were related to very inappropriate attention-seeking behaviors. Burch noticed this purple-haired young woman in her army boots watching intently each time the dogs were trained. The teenager was invited to join the training, and before long she was one of the best trainers at the shelter. Fast-forward 6 months. The shelter dogs and their trainers were invited to appear at a community event with the mayor. All of the trainers were nervous and they requested to do their demos in and among the crowd, without taking the dogs on the stage. The exception to this fear of performing in public was the transformed teenager. She wanted to be on the stage so that community leaders could see her work. Purple hair and all, she proudly walked up on the stage, and as she did, a roaring cheer came from the audience. It seemed she had invited every punk-rock fan and Goth in the northeastern United States to come and watch her. Shortly thereafter, she was hired to work at the animal shelter, where a condition of employment was to select a seminormal hair color and remove much of her facial hardware.

Clinical and educational situations are settings in which behavior analysts encounter unusual behaviors they can do something about. In these settings, when a behavior analyst is called to help, we can actually get involved in behavior replacement or the changing of habits. One area in particular has to do with dangerous aggressive, disruptive and self-injurious behaviors. One case involved a middle-aged man who was severely mentally retarded and who lived in a residential facility with eight other residents. When it came time for him to take a shower he would start screaming and throwing soap, towels, and bottles of shampoo at the staff. Not bathing was not an option, so the facility administrator would call in two additional large male "training aides." They would grab him and hold him under the shower and scrub him down. Needless to say this was ugly, and people got hurt. When the behavior analyst was called in, the situation was in crisis mode. The client's mother was very upset about the way he was being treated, one staff member was on medical leave from a back injury, and the administrator was frustrated that it took so many staff to accomplish such a small task with one client. The behavior analyst discussed the situation with everyone involved and determined all of the fighting and throwing things was the client's way of saying, "I don't want to take a shower, I hate showers, I am afraid of the shower stall, and I am afraid of slipping and falling." This client had a good history of reinforcement at this point because he regularly got his way and avoided the shower for several days. A small amount of investigation showed there was a time before all of this fighting about the shower when there wasn't a problem.

The behavior analyst proposed a replacement behavior—give the client the option of taking a bath instead.

As it turned out, when he lived at home, our client got used to taking a bath. He had his favorite rubber duckie (even though it is not age appropriate, this is true), he liked having bubbles in the water, and he had a favorite towel he liked to use. When the client was given a choice of bathing methods, he chose to have a bath. With the choice of a bath as the intervention, both the fighting and injuries were eliminated, and his mom was elated.

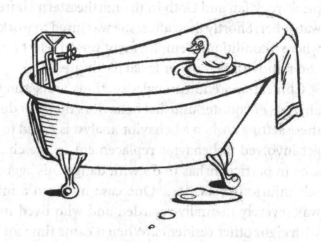

A more common use of replacement behavior comes in classroom settings in which students will routinely get up and walk away from their desk, throw their books on the floor, or hit nearby another student in an apparent fit of frustration. In these cases the children can be taught a replacement behavior that involves raising their hands or holding up a card that says, "I need a break." By teaching this replacement behavior, the teacher regains control of her classroom and the student gets some control over the schoolwork. Granted, the student may do less work within a given time, but by using a replacement behavior the student is able to signal his or her frustration and get a few minutes to calm down. Hand raising also becomes a signal to the teacher that the student needs some help understanding a difficult concept. As it turns out, teachers are much more willing to help a child who signals, "I need help," or "I need a break," than one who gets a break in the time-out corner after hitting someone.

A key to using the strategy of replacement behavior is having a good understanding of the consequences maintaining the current behavior. In the field of developmental disabilities, we have often found a severely disabled individual who is engaging in head-banging may actually be doing the behavior to get attention from caregivers. If you asked the caregivers why they are reinforcing the head-banging, they would deny they are doing so because it is not intentional on their part. But the role of the caregiver with regard to head-banging is clearly demonstrated when caregivers make their attention contingent on some other replacement behavior and the head-banging goes to zero.

Replacement behaviors can be helpful in managing the behavior of animals as well as humans. In the area of dog training, a very frequent problem new owners have with puppies is they have a tendency chew on their owners' expensive Italian leather shoes or new leather sofa. Punishment for chewing is not likely to work and can produce a neurotic puppy; the best solution is a replacement behavior. Take your puppy to a pet store and let the dog pick out a type of chew toy (not cloth) that will satisfy that urge to chew. Chewing is developmental and your dog needs to do this. For several months, you'll want to have acceptable things to chew on in every room. If your puppy looks like she is going to chew on something unacceptable, immediately take it away and give her one of her favorite chewies—it works! Another example of replacement behaviors saving the day!

• •

Key Concepts:
Replacement behavior, functions of behavior

EXERCISES:

1. What is a replacement behavior? Give an example.
2. What are some reasons young people might like to dress differently from the majority of people (e.g., Goth, all-black clothes, wearing pants with the waists near the knees, etc.)?

3. In settings for individuals with developmental disabilities, behavior analysts are called on to work on replacement behaviors. Is this a good idea? Is it better to just eliminate inappropriate behaviors?

Five

The Behavioral Take on Other Fields of Psychology

QUESTION #25.

What do behavior analysts think of counseling?
I know it is often recommended for personal
problems that people have.

Counseling is a form of treatment that relies almost entirely on talking as a means of changing behavior. There are times when people need to have someone to talk to and counseling is appropriate. For example, when children have been sexually abused, there is no doubt that counseling can be a valuable therapy.

However, when it comes to serious behavior problems, counseling is probably not the treatment of choice. Some people are in counseling for years. If you have been in counseling to work out simple problems with your spouse for 7 years and you still have "issues," there's a good chance this approach isn't working for you.

Counseling is the single most frequently recommended solution to problems of every kind by newspaper self-help columns. The distraught boyfriend writes in and says,

> I have lived with my girlfriend for two years. She is very bright and is working on her graduate degree but it seems that as time goes on, she gets on my nerves more and more often. She can be very theatrical and dramatic, using weird voices at times and always wanting to be the center of attention. Our families are eagerly awaiting a wedding. She wasn't like this when I met her, and I see things getting worse. What should I do?

The answer from the newspaper columnist: "You and your girlfriend should start couples counseling as soon as possible."
Another letter from the same column a few days later reads

> My husband has become addicted to computer games. He comes home from work, eats without saying much, and goes straight to his computer room where he stays most of the night. I never see him. If I ask him to spend time with me, he says, 'Stop whining. I need to unwind from my job.'

The answer from the newspaper columnist: "Get yourself and your husband in counseling as soon as possible."

So how would a behavior analyst who is reading these scenarios be likely to respond? For the most part, behavior analysts are skeptical of counseling to solve behavior problems such as the two mentioned previously. There's no question that there are some wonderful drug counselors, marriage counselors, and family counselors who can counsel people in some situations and help them get their lives on track. However, the main concern with advocating counseling or informal "talk therapy" for "Computer Game Widow" and "Engaged to Drama Queen" is the counseling approach may very well ignore some basic facts about human behavior.

Mr. Computer Game Addict seems to have become hooked on a very powerful reinforcer. Think about how computer games work; the same intermittent reinforcement schedule provided by slot machines is being delivered right in the comfort of his very own den. This all could have started as a function of avoidance behavior. Maybe Mr. Computer Game

Addict's wife is a nagging, unreinforcing person. Maybe she forgot to mention in her letter that she has three screaming, out-of- control children who are difficult to manage and, as a result, the house is like a war zone. Talk therapy alone is not going to change things for this couple.

Someone needs to get to the bottom of why Mr. Computer Game Addict does not want to spend time with his wife. Maybe she needs to learn to deliver a variety of reinforcers. It could be that behavior management is needed for the children so dad will not feel the need to come home from work and immediately run for cover.

How about the Academy Award-winning girlfriend? She started out okay. What happened? Mr. Tired of the Drama needs some help analyzing this. Is anyone reinforcing her? Do her friends at work find her wildly entertaining? Is she getting more and more dramatic because her boyfriend has flat affect and does not respond to her?

Many other problems frequently addressed by counselors can also be addressed with a behavior analysis approach that involves analyzing the cause of the problem and implementing a treatment plan. Behavioral researchers have used behavior analysis procedures to work with patients who have sexual disorders and sexual dysfunctions. Because of our cultural conditioning, sex is an area that can make many people uncomfortable, including some professionals trained in psychology. But this is an important part of life, and it is important to know that a behavioral approach can be used to solve this kind of

relationship problem. Another letter to a newspaper self-help columnist was from a husband who signed the letter as "Lonely in Lexington." The man bared his soul and wrote in to say he loved his wife, he tried to be a good husband, and he could not understand why she had avoided having sex with him for the past 3 years. He wanted to know if the columnist thought his wife had secretly found someone else. As with the other letters previously mentioned, the columnist recommended, "You and your wife should start counseling as soon as possible to put the sparks back in your love life."

From a behavior analysis perspective, something has gone seriously wrong in this relationship and mere talk therapy will be unlikely to change it. One possibility is all of the behaviors Romeo engaged in when they were courting are long gone. Essentially, the romance is now missing and when you take away the Hallmark cards, long-stemmed roses, and passionate "I love yous," plus all of the other behaviors that led up to sex in the beginning of a relationship (candlelight dinners, shared laughter, warm and tender hugging and snuggling, the holding of hands during a stroll in the park, compliments galore, and more) one shouldn't be surprised there is no sex now. This relationship problem is about more than sex; if they no longer have anything in common, this may be a couple that will soon be on their way to the divorce attorney's office. A couple that finds themselves in a situation like this needs to undergo a very complete analysis of their behaviors, looking at the conditions that existed when they met and were madly in love and considering those to be antecedent stimuli (actually most are antecedent behaviors) to determine what it would take to bring the romance back into their lives.

A functional assessment of Romeo's lack of lovin' could identify some other causes that have nothing to do with cards and kisses. There could be other circumstances, such as the wife having a medical problem she is embarrassed to talk about.

If marriage counselors had training in behavior analysis, they could conduct a behavioral assessment of the problems and help the troubled couple change their behavior or identify and seek treatment for medical issues. This would be a more successful approach to solving this problem.

Here's a final distinction we need to make. We aren't down on counseling. We support any type of effective treatment that helps people and has clear results. However, we have known plenty of people who have been in counseling for years and their behavior and life situations have not changed one bit. Some counselors simply talk to clients week after week about their problems. Although a sounding board is needed for people who have issues, there is a point where you need to get beyond talking and have a plan for actual behavior change. When counseling is combined with a sound functional assessment of the problem and a behavior change plan, including contingencies for the behavior changes, the chances for positive results are greatly increased. We would like to see counselors become more familiar with behavior analysis methods and perhaps team up with behavior analysts on particularly difficult cases.

● ●

Key Concepts:
Counseling, talk therapy

EXERCISES:

1. What are some situations for which traditional counseling (involving mainly listening to the client) would be appropriate?
2. What is the problem with getting only talk therapy for a behaviorally based problem?

QUESTION #26.

What do you think of the *disease model* of behavior? I've also heard this called the *medical model.*

The *disease model of behavior* (also known as the *medical model of behavior*) has become popular in the past 25 years. It is the model promoted by the medical establishment and pharmaceutical companies. Basically, by stamping certain categories of behavior problems as *diseases*, they lay claim to them for treatment purposes that can enhance their bottom line. This may seem cynical, but we believe this view has merit. Let's consider obesity, for example. Obesity involves certain behaviors that occur at too high a rate and others that occur at too low a rate. In most of the cases,

> **"In our view, obesity is actually just another behavior that needs to be analyzed in terms of contingencies of reinforcement."**

with the exception of the rare case in which there is a medical cause, the person eats too much and exercises too little. In our view, obesity is actually just another behavior that needs to be analyzed in terms of contingencies of reinforcement. Eating too much of the wrong kind of foods is a *behavior,* as is not exercising enough.

The problem in our culture is that focusing too much on the behavior can be perceived as blaming the person for their poor character and lack of willpower. Blame makes the person accountable, and for some people, blaming the person with the problem provides a quick, easy explanation as to why the problem exists.

Blame does not take into account factors such as possible medical problems, environmental issues that need to be addressed, genetic predispositions, or other more complex variables. From a behavioral perspective, we would want to work with the person to see if we can isolate the conditions under which they engage in eating and possibly figure out a way to make it a little less convenient to eat high-calorie foods (response cost) and easier to eat healthy foods. Likewise, we would want to help the person arrange his or her life in such a way that proper exercise becomes easy to do and reinforcing as well. Drugs, liposuction, and stomach stapling have significant risks and costs, and they can be avoided if someone has adequate behavioral help. Certainly, this kind of behavior change is very difficult, but surely this should be presented as the first, least-restrictive option by significant health care providers in our culture.

Smoking, alcoholism, and drug abuse are other significant classes of behavior that have also been labeled as diseases and claimed by the medical establishment. In these three cases, there is clearly a need for a tie-in with medicine because the substances involved are highly addictive and a considerable degree of counterconditioning is necessary to eliminate the powerful control by the substances. In one study it was shown that using incentives to reinforce cocaine-dependent adults for submitting cocaine-free urine samples produced a significant increase in the number of patients who completed the 24-week treatment program (Higgins et al., 1994).

Behavior analysts can play an important role in changing behavior that will result in a healthier and longer life for many people.

Key Concepts:
Disease model of behavior

EXERCISES:

1. Explain what the disease model is.
2. How could a behavior analyst work with a doctor to help someone stop smoking?
3. How could a behavior analyst work with a teenager who is overweight and lives on hamburgers, French fries, and milk shakes?

QUESTION #27.

What is the behavioral position on depression, schizophrenia, obsessive compulsive disorder and other "mental" disorders?

Behavior analysis is an approach directed specifically at operant or learned behaviors. Knowing that some forms of mental illness are biologically caused, there are absolutely times when the behavior analyst should defer to experts in the appropriate professions. However, some aspects of mild, short-term depression do appear to have a behavioral cause for which nonpharmacological treatment is recommended (United Kingdom Parliament House of Commons Health Report, 2005). An elderly, widowed pet owner who loses her furry canine companion of 15 years is very likely to go into depression in the sense of feeling deep sadness, finding no joy in other activities, having no interest in being around others, and experiencing a general feeling of being lost and abandoned. This should be expected, considering that "Snuggles" provided a significant amount of reinforcement for this individual. A dog that fills a person's life with joy—from that first kiss on the face at daybreak (along with a wagging tail that says, "let's go have some fun)" until the last walk of the evening when they share a sunset together—is going to be greatly missed. All of the behavior that was prompted and maintained by Snuggles is much less likely to occur. There is little reason to get up in the morning and no reason to go for a walk. This situation could be analyzed essentially as depression caused by the dramatic loss in reinforcement and the subsequent loss of all the behaviors maintained by that faithful, loving creature. Similar "operant depressions" can easily be seen when a person loses a job, gets divorced, or has a vintage, lovingly restored Porche stolen.

Some depression is thought to be caused by chemical deficiencies such as low levels of serotonin; evidence of this comes in the form of the use of antidepressants that increase serotonin and reduce depression. Behavior analysts respect well controlled research in any field and to the extent that severe and chronic depression can be attributed to biological causes, we would concur with this approach to what may otherwise appear to be a behavior problem. Thanks to a serious disagreement between actors Tom Cruise and Brooke Shields, one type of depression is increasingly addressed by current media. Postpartum depression is the depression that can occur up to 1 year following the birth of a child. Women who experience postpartum depression often experience symptoms such as sadness, lack of energy, trouble concentrating, anxiety, and feelings worthlessness. Postpartum depression is serious enough to affect a woman's well-being and can keep her from functioning. The most common recommended forms of treatment for postpartum depression are medications and talk therapy. Although medications may be necessary, and any woman with postpartum depression should be under the care of a medical doctor, this is an area where behavior analysts can also help. Designing individualized plans that involve getting the new mother involved in exercise, teaching her to schedule time with her partner or spouse, having her join a lunch group with other new moms, getting her to go outside every day, and teaching this new mother the skills needed to manage a screaming infant may go a long way toward offsetting the effects of postpartum depression.

Schizophrenia is another mental disorder that appears to have a biological basis. Although the behavior of a schizophrenic patient is quite bizarre and some think that elements of schizophrenia are learned, it is reasonable to believe the fundamental issue is biochemical in nature. Some research on schizophrenia points toward an imbalance of the chemical systems in the brain, specifically those involving the neurotransmitters dopamine and glutamate. This is not to say that some behavior of a schizophrenic person might be operant. However, at this time the consensus among behavior analysts is the analysis and treatment of this population is best left to those whose expertise is in the field of biochemistry.

Obsessive–compulsive disorder (OCD) clearly involves excessive, maladaptive behaviors. People with OCD have obsessions related to cleanliness, exactness, fears, and other areas. The obsessions of a person with OCD are manifested in compulsive behaviors. Examples of this would be a person who washes his hands every 10 minutes every day until the skin is raw and bleeding, a person who checks the locks on her doors exactly 25 times each and every time she leaves the house, or an adult who will not step on a crack as he walks down the sidewalk. The exact cause of OCD is not known, but it is thought to be related to heredity, brain lesions, abnormal brain glucose metabolism, or serotonergic dysfunction (Khouzam, 1999). This is another disorder in which the cause is not behaviorally based. It is difficult to believe that such strange behaviors as excessive hand washing, checking over and over again to see if a door is locked, or a powerful need to hoard or pray could be anything but operant behaviors. However, at this time there is no evidence that supports this. Behavior analysts have not typically been involved in developing treatments for OCD, but some behavior therapists have reported success with an extinction procedure referred to as "exposure and response prevention." Basically, the client is presented with the stimulus that elicits the compulsive behavior and then prevented from engaging in the behavior so that extinction can take place.

Although the treatment of some mental health problems is best left to professionals in other areas, behavior analysts can play an important role in the treatment of these populations by setting up systems-level programs to manage data, train staff, and ensure daily activities are carried out in mental health facilities.

• •

Key Concepts:
Mental disorders, depression

EXERCISES:

1. What are some mental disorders that are best treated by medical professionals? Why should behavior analysts not provide the primary treatment for people with these disorders?
2. How would a behavior analyst explain the depression that follows the death of a loved one?

QUESTION #28.

What do behavior analysts think of cognitive psychology? Do they believe in IQ? What about motivation and emotions?

The so-called cognitive revolution has not made much of an impression on most behavior analysts. As a convergence of several wildly different theoretical fields, including philosophy, cybernetics, and psycholinguistics, as well as the basic research specialties of anthropology, neuroscience, and computer science, cognitive science is about as far afield from the applied approach to behavior as one can get. For the behavior analyst, the most important things to understand are observable behavior and its relation to the environment, not the highly speculative brain processes that may underlie behavior. The field of applied cognitive psychology would appear to be a promising one for collaboration, and advances have been made in studying the reliability of eye-witness identification, techniques used by experts to master certain fields (called expertise), and the improvement of memory (Ericsson, 2002).

Behavior analysts have a different approach to studying concepts such as memory. Improving memory at a very basic level involves concepts such as stimulus discrimination. If you can never find your car keys, one approach might be to have a small basket on a table by the front door. When you come in the house, the keys are automatically dropped into the basket. By modifying the environment, you begin to get reinforced for engaging in routines or habit behaviors. With regard to more complex memory issues, behavior analysts would talk about behavioral procedures. If you are trying to teach a complex repertoire, as in, you'd like your precocious 10-year-old to become a piano virtuoso, the "memory" needed to play complex pieces of music would be taught by using shaping, chaining, and reinforcing small units of behavior.

Another area of cognitive psychology focuses on thinking, which behavior analysts have interpreted as just another, although subtle, behavior. Skinner (1957), in his difficult-to-read and greatly underappreciated work, *Verbal Behavior,* devoted a whole chapter to "Thinking," and this approach has served behavior analysts well when dealing with complex human behaviors ordinarily thought of as speech, language, communications, cognitions, or private events. One way to study these events is through a procedure called *think aloud,* which was invented by J. B. Watson, an early behaviorist (Watson, 1920). *Think aloud* is used in an updated, modern form in cognitive labs around the country (Ericsson & Simon, 1993) to study thinking and problem solving.

For the behavior analyst, cognitive behavior involves "self-talk" that might include self-instructions ("First I turn the red knob to the right, and then I pull the lever ..."), paranoid thoughts ("Oh my, they're they go talking about me again,") or other similar covert verbal behaviors such as statements of self confidence ("I know I can do this ...") that may in some way increase or decrease the likelihood of a later overt behavior. Behavior analysts are very interested in complex human behaviors but there is not a great deal of research published yet. Perhaps the most significant contribution to the general area of complex human behavior involves the recent advances in teaching language to autistic children (Sundberg & Partington, 1998). This work, which has taken the applied field of autism by storm, has become the "bible" for behavior analysts who teach language to autistic children. In what has come to be called "applied verbal behavior," these authors have shown what can be done with Skinner's concepts of verbal behavior in a very practical and necessary way. This work is supported by a body of research on language acquisition that is published in the peer-reviewed journal *Analysis of Verbal Behavior.*[11]

Behavior analysts are not involved with standardized testing so they don't make much use of IQ scores. We are, however, very much interested in knowing about an individual's level of practical functioning if this will help us develop effective behavioral programs. As members of habilitation teams, behavior analysts are often involved with conducting

---

[11]Published by the Association for Behavior Analysis: International. To see recent topics go to: www.abainternational.org/avbjournal/currentissue.asp

assessments of adaptive behavior. Does this person have any leisure skills? Can she wash her hair? Can this young client with developmental disabilities feed himself with a spoon? These are functional, real-world behaviors that are needed to get through the day.

One topic that is very much at the heart of behavior analysis has to do with motivation. You might even say that we consider motivation to be a prime focus of the field, and we consider it a topic that is present in almost every study of behavior. For behavior analysts, motivation has to do with reinforcement and reinforcement has to do in a major way with deprivation; that is, unless the subject has some deprivation of the reinforcer, then basically there is no reason for the behavior to occur. Jack Michael of Western Michigan University introduced the expression *establishing operation* (Michael, 1982) as a term to help behavior analysts describe, understand, predict, and control behavior. In 2003, in a major theoretical article, Michael and his colleagues (Laraway, Snycerski, Michael, & Poling, 2003) suggested using the more generic term *motivating operation* to describe environmental events that influence the effects of operant consequences. With the term *motivation* as a centerpiece of operant theory, it is clear that behavior analysts consider understanding what motivates people to engage in certain behaviors a paramount feature of our field.

> **"It is clear that behavior analysts consider understanding what motivates people to engage in certain behaviors a paramount feature of our field."**

Jack Michael

As we mentioned earlier, the first question that a behavior analyst asks on being presented with a behavior problem is "Why? Why does the behavior occur? What are the

> **" The first question that a behavior analyst asks is 'Why? Why does the behavior occur?' "**

controlling variables?" When we understand what motivates a person to engage in a behavior, we can then proceed to develop an ethical and effective behavior plan.

As behavior analysts we do not usually target emotions or emotional behavior, but that does not mean that we are not concerned with emotions. The behavioral position is that emotions accompany certain behaviors and certainly result from consequences, but emotions alone are probably not responsible for behavior. We suggest focusing on the environmental change that produced the troubling emotion. A person who is sad or angry feels that way for some reason. Something has happened to cause this feeling and we are concerned about this; we don't like to see a person being miserable in this condition. Focusing too long on the emotion itself can be a major distraction from identifying the cause. Behavior analysts generally discount programs to enhance feelings such as the failed 1986 California Task Force on the Importance of Self-Esteem (Foxx & Roland, 2005).

The goal of this program was to improve reading by enhancing the "feelings of self-esteem" in school children. There are other similar programs such as programs in anger management that do not deal with the cause of the anger. Learning to breathe deeply, count to 100 slowly, or play mind games with yourself avoids what could be a serious impediment to happiness. As an example, when a person is extremely angry over a work situation (let's say the person is being discriminated against by her sexist boss), counseling for anger management may not be the best solution. Such situations are complex and, depending on the specifics of the situation, there are several ways that this can be handled. One solution would be to file a complaint against the boss with Human Resources. Depending on the nature of the comments, another solution might be to give feedback to the boss along with shaping appropriate behavior. As behavior analysts, we would like to see people be more analytical about their feelings and would urge them to learn how to determine what the causal variables are and make the necessary adjustments to produce more desirable outcomes and feelings.

Most of the time, changing the way one thinks about things will not fix problems. The solution does not involve a cognitive process; it involves having a plan of action and changing behavior. The new bride feels trapped in her marriage. The day her daddy spent $60,000 for a fairy-tale wedding, she was certain her life was going to be idyllic. Now, only a few months into her marriage, she has the startling realization that her princess days are over. Her husband is more committed to his work and is constantly traveling and giving her very little time. If this young woman is starting to feel lonely and sad, she has good reason; she does not need Prozac, group therapy, nor does she necessarily need to change her thoughts. She needs to make some changes in her life and arrange for more reinforcing consequences to improve her situation and her emotional well-being.

> **"Behavior analysts use emotions and emotional behavior as indicators of satisfactory or unsatisfactory contingencies of reinforcement in a person's life ..."**

Behavior analysts use emotions and emotional behavior as indicators of satisfactory or unsatisfactory contingencies of reinforcement in a person's life; they are important and a key to understanding what needs to be done to help the person improve their condition.

Key Concepts:
Cognitive psychology, motivation, emotions

EXERCISES:

1. Look at any recent general psychology text and review the section on
   cognitive psychology; see if you can find examples of applied cognitive
   studies that might appear to overlap with applied behavior analysis.
2. How do behavior analysts talk about motivation?
3. What role does understanding someone's emotions play in behavioral
   treatment?

Basic Skepticism

QUESTION #29.
You seem so skeptical of other approaches. Can you tell me why?

Several years ago, at a meeting of the Association for Behavior Analysis in San Francisco, a speaker caught the attention of the behavioral audience when she reported on "some amazing findings" from her work with autistic youths. She had been trying a brand new technique called "facilitated communication" (FC) with teenage autistic clients, and, in her words, she "was simply blown away" by what she had found. Why, they really weren't autistic at all but rather were normal people trapped by their inability to communicate. All they needed was a little help. From a facilitator. A facilitator who would sit next to them and guide their hands as they typed out messages on a keyboard. The audience was enthralled, but many were thinking, "What? This doesn't sound right. You're telling us that these young people who have never shown any acquisition of expressive language are writing poems? We don't believe it." Despite this, it was a compelling story, and there were people (who had been trained in behavior analysis) crying when she finished reading some of the poems (which were quite good by anyone's standards).

What was missing from this presentation was any actual data of any kind, except for a typed poem. By the way, the poem had no spelling errors, no typos, and no grammatical errors. This is kind of amazing, considering that there are plenty of college students who have been educated for 25 years who can't produce work as clean as the sample poem we were viewing.

If there is one thing we can learn from our friends who are skeptics, it's that extraordinary claims require extraordinary proof. This was truly the time to apply this standard but no proof was offered and, surprisingly, none was asked for in the question and answer period.

Over the next few years the momentum built surrounding FC. The technique was also used with adults and children with cerebral palsy, who reportedly, through FC, could now write letters to their parents, take math tests, and write short stories. Although many nonverbal individuals with mild mental retardation and cerebral palsy may have the receptive language needed to make choices about how a story should end or what color of paint should be used in a picture, what is at question is the ability of people who have never written a poem or story to suddenly produce one that includes sophisticated concepts, vocabulary, and language.

The popularity of FC grew until there were more and more dramatic instances of successful breakthroughs; autistic children and youths all over the country were taking regular classes with their facilitators in tow, and school systems were footing the bill. Many experts in autism became skeptical and began designing research using scientific methods to actually test this magical cure. Lo and behold, FC was a—drum roll please—hoax.

It turns out that with FC it was actually the facilitators who were writing the poems and the letters and doing the homework. In the end, it was made abundantly clear in a TV documentary produced by the Public Broadcast System's *Frontline.* "Prisoners of Silence" produced by Jon Palfreman (1993), clearly showed when an autistic student was exposed to one stimulus and the facilitator to another, what got typed is what the facilitator saw. It was dramatic and convincing. The facilitators who were the test participants were visibly shaken, and shortly after, many left the profession for other lines of work. Although there may have been some innocent, well intended professionals who were sucked in and believed that FC could

"Behavior analysts are skeptical. We like to refer to our skepticism as critical thinking."

help people communicate, there was absolutely no hard evidence for this procedure, which ironically was being pushed at workshops all over the country.

Critical thinking can be applied to most claims about behavior that just don't sound right. Radical changes in behavior don't usually sound right. Reports of people engaging in behavior where there are no obvious consequences don't sound right. We know how behavior change comes about. It is not an easy process and it takes a lot of  observation and analysis. This can be time consuming, first just to understand what the controlling variables are, and then to figure out how to produce some meaningful behavior change. Behavior analysts are skeptical of infomercials that promise "Five Simple Steps to Financial Freedom"; "magic pills" for dramatic weight loss; very expensive, strange diets that supposedly cure autism; or therapies that work without any scientific basis, visible means, or mechanisms for working. "Thought field therapy," for example, supposedly works by "cosmic energy from the cosmos ... transmitted to a person through the channel of an accomplished healer." (Jacobson, Foxx, & Mulick, 2005, p. 149). Now, does that sound crazy or what? What kind of person could possibly take such a preposterous claim seriously? Certainly not one with any critical thinking skills.

Although we do not claim to have cornered the market on the treatment for autism, what behavior analysis does claim is the corner on evidence-based treatments that have passed muster with the leading scientific, peer-reviewed journals. Our critical thinking also applies to approaches that have been endorsed by well respected figures, including past presidents, football coaches, and entertainment icons. Son-Rise Program® is just such a treatment approach that behavior analysts would be quite skeptical of primarily for its lack of an empirical basis and potentially for its strong association with other questionable fad-like treatments such as auditory integration therapy, vitamin therapy, sensory integration, and the highly questionable gluten/casein free diet. Although vitamins and diets free of gluten may result in some health benefits, the point to remember is that there is no empirical evidence that such diets cure children who are autistic.

● ●

Key Concepts:
Skepticism, critical thinking, FC

EXERCISES:

1. Describe some treatments for autism for which there are no controlled studies.
2. As a behavior analyst, when you hear about a procedure that supposedly impacts behavior, what are some questions you should ask about the procedure?
3. What is FC? What does the most current controlled research show about FC?

QUESTION #30.
What is the behavioral position on freedom and free will?

"Free will" is the ability to select a particular course of action to fulfill a need or desire. Whether we have free will has been debated for centuries. The ability to control our own destiny or things happening because of fate are ideas that sometimes accompany the debate about free will. There are deep philosophical divides among scholars on this important issue.

For the behavior analyst, this is a practical question that comes down to how we approach our daily life and how we try to help others with theirs. People who are under a great deal of aversive control—the child of a domineering, abusive father; the husband of a nagging spouse; a saleswoman who has constant pressure to meet deadlines only to discover even more unreachable goals have been set by management—are people who might feel as though they have little or no freedom. They could run away from home, divorce the spouse, or quit the job, but these may not be realistic options at the moment. As well educated persons, if we can see that these situations are bad, we might be able to chart a course to freedom from all of this aversiveness.

As behavior analysts, we see ourselves as being in an ideal position to accomplish this important goal and we do this for a living, minus all of the philosophical baggage. We know that aversive control produces escape and avoidance behavior. It can elicit aggression and cause bad feelings in those living under these insufferable conditions.

To get the ball rolling, the person living under aversive conditions must seek help from someone who understands what it will take to solve the problem. This does not take willpower but rather enough insight into the condition to see that it does not need to be permanent. There needs to be some initial behavior to reverse the conditions. These are skills that can be taught and should be taught to every person approaching adulthood. Behavior analysts support and promote assertiveness training as a method of breaking the chain that is keeping anyone in a situation where the person is constrained emotionally or physically by direct or implied threats of harm.

Control by aversive events is fairly obvious, and we take it as a serious obligation to work with our clients to remove these barriers to a happy and productive life. Another, more subtle challenge to freedom is that which comes from schedules of reinforcement, specifically intermittent schedules of reinforcement. Intermittent schedules can lock people into certain patterns of behavior (such as gambling) that are destructive and harmful to individuals and those around them.

As we discussed earlier, computer games pose this sort of threat to freedom because they can provide a type of reinforcement that may be far more powerful than what can be derived in the real world. This is especially the case if the person feels powerless in a job or domestic situation and can retreat to a world of make-believe where he can control some consequences and where the intermittent reinforcers make life interesting (at least for a couple of hours). It is not useful to say a person addicted to computer games has the free will to discontinue this activity because it flies in the face of what we know about contingencies of reinforcement. Intermittent schedules of reinforcement (variable interval, variable ratio) can take away a person's freedom just as surely as a controlling boss or domineering spouse.

As behavior analysts, we are committed to trying to enrich the lives of the people with whom we work. We would like to see people enjoy the reinforcers that come from friends and family, as well as from those that have been produced by our culture, such as art, literature, and sports. All of these reinforcers, along with those in nature, give people the freedom to come into contact with a wide range of reinforcers. To this extent, we would say these people have more freedom than those who are not in a position to make choices to experience these reinforcers. Someone in a working relationship with a controlling boss or a living arrangement with a domineering spouse has far less freedom than is desirable. Behavior analysts believe it is important to have an expansive repertoire to maximize one's reinforcers, and this involves many choices of behaviors and reinforcers.

Behavior analysts, for all their interest in promoting a good life full of lots of interesting behaviors and reinforcers, are still determinists. We do not believe that people are free to engage in just any behavior they like; we do believe that behavior is controlled by its consequences. Understanding that behavior is controlled by its consequences will help everyone understand how important it is to be able to analyze their condition, to do a personal audit so to speak, and to determine if they are satisfied with their choices. The act of choosing is an operant behavior just like any other behavior. The extent to which we, as behavior analysts, can contribute to strengthening this key behavior is the extent to which we can expand the freedoms that will make live worthwhile for everyone.

●●

Key Concepts:
Free will, choice, aversive events

EXERCISES:

1. How do behavior analysts view free will?
2. Give an example of how choice can help a person escape an aversive situation.

QUESTION #31.

What is your standard of proof? What I mean is, what does it take for you to believe that a treatment or procedure is effective?

Behavior analysts have a very high bar for proof that a certain variable actually is responsible for a designated change in behavior. Probably the most important criterion is that there be a clear demonstration of experimental control, that is, when the treatment is applied, the behavior changes, and when it is withdrawn, the behavior returns to its initial level. This demonstration needs to be made more than once and with several participants.[12] In addition, we need a number of other factors to be in play. We require an operational definition of the treatment (the independent variable) and data to show it was applied precisely as specified. Once there has been a data-based demonstration of a relationship between an independent and dependent variable (i.e., a cause–effect relationship) it is further necessary for there to be replication of the findings by other behavioral scientists working in separate labs or applied settings. There are quite a few other requirements too numerous to go into here (see Bailey & Burch, 2002, for details) but needless to say, fascinating anecdotes and heartwarming stories are far below the bar of proof.

The fantastic story of an autistic boy "cured" when his parents decided to mimic his stereotyped behavior does not rise to the level of proof required for behavior analysts. Also not meeting the standard of proof are anecdotal reports, case studies, or uncontrolled experiments. Reports that certain diets can change autistic behavior do not meet our need for evidence-based treatment. This might seem like a very conservative standard, and it is. Like most scientists, we are skeptical of "amazing results" and "unheard of, dramatic outcomes" often touted by those who would prey on parents and the public, who are desperate for a magic to cure autism, mental illness, or sleepless nights.

---

[12]As an alternative, behavior analysts also accept clear demonstrations of experimental control shown via the multiple-baseline design.

We know it is easy to fool people into believing most anything as the Amazing Randi has shown over and over in his replications of "psychic surgery" (see www.randi.org) and other hoaxes. The placebo effect (Park, 2000) accounts for many of the unscientific beliefs that people have about a wide variety of treatments with no known scientific foundation (Singer & Lalich, 1996). Rebirthing, aromatherapy, past-life regression, neruo-linguistic programming, FC, and eye movement desensitization reprocessing, sensory integration therapy, and dozens of other approaches simply have no basis in empirical, scientific fact. It is startling to learn, for example, that a recent survey of occupational therapists showed that 82% always use sensory integration although there is not a single, well controlled study demonstrating its efficacy (Smith, Mruzek, & Mozingo, 2005).

As behavior analysts, we take comfort in knowing that literally hundreds of well controlled studies have been published in the *Journal of Applied Behavior Analysis* and other journals in the past 30 years, validating even the smallest elements of our treatment methods.

• •

Key Concepts:
Standard of proof, cause–effect relationship, placebo effect, evidence-based treatment

EXERCISES:

1. What do behavior analysts mean by "standard of proof"?
2. Watch for infomercials on television. What sort of proof do they present for their product or service? Did they present actual scientific data?
3. What if you do believe that aromatherapy makes you feel better? How could you prove that this works? Is there an experiment that could be designed if you had access to a lab and some researchers?

Chapter Seven

Myths and the Media

QUESTION #32.

Some people refer to reinforcement as a form of bribery. Do you agree with that?

Absolutely not. *Bribery* is "the offering of money or other incentives to persuade somebody to do something, especially something dishonest or illegal" (Encarta® World English Dictionary, 1999). Behavior analysts abhor the notion that a powerful generalized positive reinforcer such as money would be used to persuade someone to engage in dishonest or illegal behavior. We do like the idea of using powerful generalized reinforcers to strengthen appropriate behaviors. Many parents who have difficulty convincing their children to complete school homework use money as a reinforcer for getting the work done on time. Others may provide a bonus for grades when report cards come due. In neither case is money used as a bribe because the target behavior is highly appropriate. Another feature of bribes, which the dictionary does not mention, is that with bribes reinforcement is usually given in advance, as an incentive for the illegal behavior. As you know by now, reinforcers are always made contingent on, that is, they follow a behavior. We discourage the idea of holding up the reinforcer as an antecedent for behavior.

We've all witnessed scenes like this in the grocery store: "Mommy, I want that, right there, I want it. I want it." This 4-year-old cutie-pie is standing in the grocery basket pointing at the sugar-coated cereal she saw on a children's television show. Mom initially refused, saying in a matter-of-fact voice, "No, not today, you don't need that. We already have cereal."

Scene Two: "Please, please, Mommy, I want it! I want it!" Now she's screaming and crying. Several customers pause to see what is going on, mom takes a quick look around and sees the gathering crowd. There is more crying, and cutie-pie now looks like she might be holding her breath. Mom gives up, saying, "Okay, okay, if you stop crying and sit down, I'll get it for you, but you have to stop crying."

Scene Three: Our little moppet is sitting in the cart eating the cereal. Quietly. With a satisfied little grin on her face that says, "There, I showed you who's boss." In this case the food was used as a bribe, not that ceasing the crying was an illegal behavior, but mom essentially promised a reward, under duress, to stop an aversive event. You might ask what mom should have done under the circumstances. The way this should be

handled may be awkward, but sometimes parents must swallow their pride and do what is in the best behavioral interest of their children. In this case, when the screaming and wailing started, mom should have taken her little darling out of the store (saying to the nearest clerk "I'll be right back to finish my shopping"), not talking to her daughter at all, just walking briskly straight to the car. Then she should have put the little screamer in the carseat and let her go at it until she stopped. Although it is hard to do this, mom needs to maintain her composure and not show any signs of anger or emotion. Then, as soon as the child is calm and quiet, it's back to the store and right down that same cereal aisle again. If cutie-pie repeats her tantrum, it's back to the car. It shouldn't take more than two or three repetitions for her to get it. On future trips, mom could establish the rules before they leave the house, "We're going shopping in a little while. I want you to be good today, no asking for anything and no crying. If you cry, we will leave the store. If you are a good little shopper and help Mommy, you can watch *Sesame Street* when we get home." This is the appropriate way to use reinforcers: When they are planned in advance by the parent—who sets the rules and who will not be blackmailed into giving a bribe to a screaming child.

●●

Key Concepts:
Reinforcement as bribery, bribes

EXERCISES:

1. What are bribes? How is a bribe different from a reinforcer?
2. You are at a social gathering. Someone finds out you are a behavior analyst. He or she says, "So do you believe in paying off kids for doing their chores and things like that? I think all these new childrearing techniques are ridiculous. We did our chores because we had to. I don't think you should bribe kids with money and toys to do what they are supposed to do." How would you respond?

QUESTION #33.

If you use behavioral procedures like food treats and tokens with your kids, will they get to where they only work for reinforcers?

There is really no reason for this to happen unless the parents mismanage behavior programs for their children. One very important rule of positive reinforcement with children and adults is it is important to fade the tangible reinforcers in favor of the natural consequences of the behavior.

When it came using behavior procedures, Pauline was a grandmother who was a natural. When her daughter had to enter a residential treatment program for substance abuse, Pauline began raising Gregory and Garrett, her 5- and 6-year-old grandsons. Pauline had some in-home behavioral services when her grandsons were first moved into her home and, with the assistance and oversight of a behavior analyst, Pauline learned how to teach new skills, use reinforcement, set up a very basic token system and use the Premack Principle (also known as Grandma's rule). The basic premise of the Premack Principle is that a preferred activity can be used to reinforce a less-favored activity.

Pauline decided that the boys needed to learn some basic household chores. After learning about "Grandma's Rule" from the behavior analyst, she started by having them clean up their rooms to gain access to other reinforcers: clean up your room and you can go outside; clean up your room and you can come down to dinner; clean up your room and you can watch TV or go outside to play. That went fairly well, and the boys learned the routine in a few weeks. Pauline went to work one day and announced to her friends she was going to teach the boys to do their own laundry. Her coworkers (many who couldn't get their spouses to do laundry) laughed and said, "Good luck."

In the first session to teach Garrett and Gregory to use the washing machine, Pauline discovered they could not reach the controls. She took the boys to the store and let them choose a small stepstool for doing the laundry. Then came the hands-on instructions and the step-by-step training with Pauline modeling the behaviors and the boys practicing. When each boy completed his first load of laundry, Pauline gave him a quarter. In the beginning, Pauline was present every time the children used the washer and dryer, but she was eventually able to fade her presence. Before long, the boys washed their own clothes, and instead of getting a quarter each time, Pauline transitioned them to a small weekly allowance.

Throughout the entire process, as the boys learned new skills, Pauline praised the quality of their work, bragged about them to friends and neighbors, and let them know how proud she was that they were growing into fine young men who could be counted on to help out when needed.

Because there are many possible ways to mess up a system like this, such as not fading out the money very gradually or not pairing the money with praise, formal behavior programs should not be conducted without a Board Certified Behavior Analyst or Board Certified Associate Behavior Analyst.

When people are opposed to behavior programs, a common objection is that the individuals for whom the behavior program is designed are receiving preferential treatment. "It's not fair," a teacher will tell us. "The rest of the class doesn't have a chance to earn candy or extra free time." Even when working with adults in business settings, the concept of using money and fading programs is hard for many people to understand. Supervisors will say, "So you take away the prizes and then what?"

As behavior analysts, when we work with people, we need to stress that the ultimate goal of behavior programming is to produce adaptive behavior that is maintained by natural reinforcers. We use points, money, candy, and other tangible reinforcers because sometimes the only way to get someone to do something is for a greater payoff. These contrived reinforcers are used to jump-start a program. With weight loss, for every specified number of pounds lost, the person might get a new item of clothing. However, although the ultimate reinforcer should be looking and feeling better, it does not come instantly, and the use of other reinforcers can be extremely helpful.

The main thing to remember is that anyone who decides to use tangible rewards should start with a plan in mind for eventually fading them for naturally occurring reinforcers.

● ●

Key Concepts:
Premack Principle, "Grandma's Rule," token system, natural reinforcers

EXERCISES:

1. You have been asked by a parent how she can get her 8-year-old son, who hates homework, to get his homework done before 10 p.m. By then, she is frustrated and yelling at him. What are some basic suggestions you could give?
2. What is the Premack Principle?
3. Is it appropriate to use token systems (or token economies) with young children? If you had a 7-year-old who had a basic chore list that included cleaning her bedroom, doing her homework, and cleaning the hamster cage every day, how could you use a token system for these behaviors? What would you do first?

QUESTION #34.

I heard that Skinner raised his children in a box and that they became mentally ill and that one sued him. Is this true?

No, it's not true, but rumors like this persist because those who are opposed to Skinner's ideas want to believe that he would do such a thing. Unfortunately, there are people in this world who are either ignorant of the facts or happy to pass along rumors (Slater, 2004).

Here's what is true: Skinner built a special "air crib" for his second daughter Deborah (who is alive and well and living in London as a successful artist) that was enclosed and climate controlled. He did this at a time when houses in the northeast had high ceilings; heat rises, and the rooms were cold. Heat was expensive, and it seemed like a waste to Skinner to have to heat an entire room when a baby slept in a very small space. As an infant, Deborah napped in the crib for a few hours each day and it served as her own personal bedroom at night for the first couple of years of her life. She grew up normal and healthy, not having a cold until she was 6 years old. The air crib was designed to eliminate "the worst aspects

Deborah Skinner as an infant.

of a baby's typical sleeping arrangements: clothes, sheets and blankets. These not only have to be washed, but they restrict arm and leg movement and are a highly imperfect method of keeping a baby comfortable" (Buzan, 2004, p. 2). As an adult, Deborah reports having very little knowledge of her first 2½ years and certainly was not adversely affected by her time spent in the air crib (Buzan, 2004).

First author Jon Bailey's two sons also slept in an air crib that was purchased from Mont Wolf. Wolf also used the air crib for his two children. They were healthy, normal children and adults. It is a myth that the child lives in the air crib all day. It is used for the same period of time during the day and night that a regular crib is used. The air crib performed exactly as Skinner said it did. It perfectly controlled the climate year round, it eliminated the need for blankets, and there was a great deal of peace of mind knowing an infant was not going to suffocate or get his head caught in the bars as might be possible with a normal crib.

As for the misconceptions about the air crib, one problem might have come from the fact that people use the language, "Skinner's kids were raised in an air crib." "Raised in an air crib" sounds like they were brought home from the hospital, put in their "box" and left there until it was time to send them off to college. Perhaps a better way to talk about the air crib would be to say, "the child slept and napped in a climate controlled crib."

Second author Mary Burch was giving a presentation on using behavioral procedures with infants when a member of the audience raised her hand to ask a question. In a voice that had an edge to it, the indignant woman asked, "Do you know anything about the box that Skinner raised his children in? How did they get the baby's food in there?"

Another professional told us an air crib story. This person attended a business management workshop where the presenter talked about the importance of human relationships. The speaker went on to say there were psychology "studies" where the experimenter raised his daughter in a box and she developed abnormally. The speaker joked, "Where was this girl's mother in all of this?"

Unfortunately, among people outside of behavior analysis, B. F. Skinner was one of the most misunderstood figures in the history of psychology. He was never into marketing or being slick. He was a scientist. It is really too bad that he didn't have a professional sidekick who was a marketing whiz. If the air crib had been given a cute name, had bunnies painted on it, and had been sold to a major manufacturer of infant furniture, its use might have been more widespread. Basically, the idea is still a good one. Provide heat and air-conditioning to maintain a perfectly controlled temperature in the space the baby needs for sleeping, avoid heavy blankets and clothing that could cause suffocation during the winter, and buffer all the noise in the house so the infant can sleep.

The air crib examples, along with other false impressions about behavior analysis, point to our responsibility as behavior analysts to correct misconceptions and play a part in the accurate dissemination of information pertaining to our field.

• •

Key Concepts:
Air crib, Skinner's children

EXERCISES:

1. What is an air crib? Explain the purpose of the air crib and why Skinner developed it.
2. When parents used air cribs with their babies, how much time did the child spend in the air crib? Were they raised in it?

QUESTION #35.

I saw Dr. Phil on TV one time and he sounded sort of like a behaviorist. He was talking about consequences of behavior and taking responsibility. He's known for asking, "How's that working for you?" What do you think of him?

First author, Jon Bailey, writes:

D r. Phil McGraw is a marketing genius who works with the best public relations people in the business. Backed initially by Oprah Winfrey, he took the world by storm with his jovial Texas drawl, his seeming directness, and his warmth and sincerity. His degree is in psychology; his specialty was in behavioral medicine and rumor has it that he took a behavioral psychology course at the University of North Texas, where he earned his PhD. He is not specifically trained as a behavior analyst, and it shows. Most of the time Dr. Phil comes across as a commonsense, compassionate, and blunt individual who likes to throw out catchphrases that sound sort of behavioral, "How's that workin for ya'?" being one of the most famous. He tends to dramatize the problems people have using staged video clips that are repeated at the beginning of each segment following a commercial break (about every 6 minutes or so). There is a build-up with teasers to keep the viewers glued to their TV sets, "When we come back, Julie tells us a secret she's never told anyone, and it explains why she has no backbone."

People report they think Dr. Phil is a behaviorist because he occasionally suggests what appear to be behavioral procedures. He emphasizes the need for children to come into contact with consequences and supports a sort of benign authoritarian model of parenting. On most days, the cases that make it to his stage are so dramatic it's easy to see what the solutions are and many of them are behavioral but vague. For example (Casey et al., 2005)

You have exactly 50% of what it takes to take charge in this family and get Montanna under control. [Montanna was a 4-year-old who ruled the roost with her screaming fits and aggressive behavior.] You dearly love your children; that's very important. Now you need the other 50%—a plan. And I'm going to give you that plan when we come back.

When he comes back Dr. Phil repeats the footage we've already seen two or three times and now the parents are sitting in the audience waiting for "The Plan." Dr. Phil says,

You need to strip her room of everything including the TV, the video games, the bed, everything. You take everything away but the minimum, a mattress on the floor. Now she has to earn everything back. She will scream, but you won't give in. She will whine and plead but she gets nothing back until she asks for it nicely and politely, do you understand?

The parents, with dazed eyes staring at their guru, nod "yes," they understand, they will strip the room, they won't give in, they promise. Does this sound like 1960s style behavior modification to you? It does to me, and there is essentially no behavior analysis in Dr. Phil's approach. It's dramatic and draconian, but it's not the way a behavior analyst would approach the problem. And, if this is all the parents are going to get, we'd predict that it's going to fail. Miserably. As a concept, the notion that you will strip a 4-year-old of all her worldly possessions and then make her earn them back sounds like good advice, but how are the parents to carry this out exactly? How much good behavior does Montanna have to engage in? What if she gets a few things back and then falls back into her old routine? Without someone there to help them through what could be a mighty big conflict, we doubt that the parents will be able to navigate these troubled waters alone. Perhaps the most perplexing aspect of this particular show (Casey et al., 2005) was that the film clips, when viewed carefully, do not show that Montanna was at all responding to possessions as related to her severe tantrums. She wasn't interested in watching TV or playing with video games. The video clips clearly show that Montanna was aggressive related to not getting her way, to not being the center of attention, and that it was primarily the mother's attention that she was seeking. In other words, Dr. Phil, because he was not a behavior analyst, did not see what was very obvious from his own film clips. Mom would make a request, "Montanna it's time to pick up your toys." Montanna says, "Nooo," and raises her hand with a toy in it threatening mom, then a loud scream, and mom leaves the room. In another clip, two children are playing together ignoring Montanna. She comes up with a toy and hits one right in the face. The child falls over and starts crying; mom comes in from off camera and grabs Montanna. Cut. "When we come back, I'll tell you what we're going to do about this. Don't turn that dial."

Second author, Mary Burch, writes:

There are 50 questions in *How to Think Like a Behavior Analyst*. As authors, we agree on the answers to every single question but this one. Dr. Phil is a good guy. Nope, he doesn't take data on his show and he doesn't use words like *functional analysis*. And it is true that he doesn't always look for the cause of the behavior. But here's what he has done. He's managed to get the American public interested in thinking about behavior. He talks about solving behavior problems in a matter-of-fact

way and is finding solutions that work. He refers people to state-of- the-art treatment programs. He does explain behavioral concepts so people can understand them, "Well, you understand she's doin' that because there is some pay-off." He talks about time-out and explains that if the child is being sent to a bedroom full of toys and electronic gadgets, she has not been sent to time-out. Dr. Phil may be bringing us "Behavior Lite," but by golly, he's bringing it to millions of people.

Dr. Phil has brought the topic of behavior to the public and that is something we as behavior analysts have failed at miserably. About 15 years ago, at the Association for Behavior Analysis conference, Paul Chance encouraged behavior analysts to take our message to mass media outlets in addition to the scientific journals. We haven't done it yet. As behavior analysts, we spend too much time preaching to the converted. Far too few of us have been media trained. You can't go on television or the radio with a crying parent and talk to her about stimulus control and the contingencies of reinforcement and expect to be invited back. Dr. Phil has taken a very important first step and, although he may not adhere to the experimental rigor we would like, as a field, we have a lot to learn from him. Tell me that Dr. Phil has not made a significant contribution and I have only one response. As the bald guy from Texas says, "That dog won't hunt."

● ●

Key Concepts:
Dr. Phil, media training

EXERCISES:

1. Watch an episode of Dr. Phil. What are the behavior problems discussed on the day you watch the show? Can you identify any behavioral solutions offered by Dr. Phil?
2. Read an article in the *Journal of Applied Behavior Analysis*. If you were hired as a media consultant, how would you write a press release to report the findings to the general public?
3. Select an article on autism from a behavioral journal. Describe (you don't have to actually do this) how you would rewrite the scientific article and the points you would cover if you were to submit this article to *Parenting Magazine*.

QUESTION #36.
Is the "Supernanny" just a behavior analyst with a British accent?

S *upernanny* is a new hit reality show on ABC that first aired in Britain in 2004. For those who have seen the show, the Supernanny does indeed appear to use behavioral procedures with the out-of-control children she confronts weekly in prime time. For those who haven't seen the show, it goes like this: Jo Frost, the Supernanny, visits a well off suburban family with two to four out-of-control children. She observes the dynamics of the family routine (good) and makes "mental notes." Unfortunately, no data are taken, except for the occasional behavior chart data. Then she sits the parents down for a chat in the evening to spell out what she's seen and to describe what they will need to do to gain control over their family and have a peaceful life. Typically, the parents are loving and well meaning, but they talk too much ("I don't want to tell you again, you are making Mommy angry, please don't hit your little brother with that car …"), have no clue about consequences and how they work, and they apologize constantly to their bratty kids, who do indeed call the shots. The parents actually appear to be afraid of these "monsters" (as they are often referred to by these frustrated moms and dads).

What Jo Frost has in spades is loads of charm, British wit, self-confidence, and a bluntness that startles the parents and makes for great TV close-ups of the reactions on their faces when told that they will have to change everything they are doing; "No parents are perfect," they are assured, "We'll start tomorrow." The Supernanny typically starts with a posted daily schedule as a means of signaling when important daily activities like mealtime, playtime, and bedtime will occur, and then Frost sets out to tackle the most important dysfunctional behaviors. Her directions are clear, and she role-plays how she wants the parents to apply "The Naughty Spot." The Naughty Spot is Supernanny's version of time-out, and it follows the rule of 1 minute in time-out for each year of the child's age. She also uses ignoring (extinction for bad behavior) and prompting of appropriate behaviors. The Supernanny uses just a few procedures, shows the parents how to apply them throughout the day, and gives good feedback.

What Frost is missing, totally missing, is any sense of explaining the functions that the tantrum, defiant, and aggressive behaviors have for these troublesome tykes. As with Dr. Phil, the Supernanny has dumbed down behavior management to the simple matter of control by using consequences. She's also big on apologies—"Tell your brother that you are sorry you hit him." She makes no attempt to show the parents how to look for functions for the behaviors so they might have a better understanding of how they got in the fix in which they find themselves. She also makes no attempt to teach the parents anything about the basic principles; for her it's all just "details" and consistency. Without any theory, no data except for the visual record and behavior chart, and a gross  violation of confidentiality, it is hard to even compare the Supernanny with a behavior analyst. However, if one of our own were to take over an episode, it probably would not make very good prime time viewing. A good behavior analyst would want to do a functional assessment of the target behaviors, teach the basic principles to the parents, and drop the "1 minute per year" rule for time-out. Further, there would be a much more systematic use of reinforcers, which play a surprisingly little role in the Supernanny's scheme of things, and the half-hearted apologies would be gone.

Key Concepts:
Supernanny, time-out, extinction, prompting, causes of behavior

EXERCISES:

1. With notepad in hand, watch an episode of *Supernanny* and see if you can observe the consequences that are maintaining the target behaviors.
2. Note the use of training in how to apply social reinforcers with the children.
3. Go to the *Journal of Applied Behavior Analysis* Web site and look up some of the behaviors that you have observed and see if you can find a relevant article on the evidence-based treatment of the problem.

Eight

Getting Started in a Career in Behavior Analysis

QUESTION #37.

What exactly is the job of a behavior analyst and what are the educational requirements? I'm not sure what degree I should get in graduate school.

The job of the behavior analyst is complex and multifaceted. Jobs vary a great deal, depending on who the employer is and who the client is. For example, if you are working for a consulting firm, you may work with two to five different families or schools each week. If you were hired by a school system, you might be working with just as many different teachers each week. If you were working for a family, you might work with two or three different children on different problems. The behavior analyst's primary job in any case is to gather a great deal of information about the client. Then, the behavior analyst will try to discover how severe the problem behavior is, how long it has been going on, and what variables are maintaining the behavior. Once this is done, the behavior analyst then typically identifies the relevant people in the client's environment and will demonstrate the treatment (always approved by the key people) that has been developed. After demonstrating the treatment, the behavior analyst will coach the relevant "mediators" through the proper implementation of the intervention. Data will be taken before intervention to determine a baseline of the performance, during the intervention to make sure it is effective, and after the intervention is completed to make sure that the program is properly implemented and that it works over time. Behavior analysts must follow a rigorous and detailed code of ethics (Bailey & Burch, 2005) throughout this entire process to make sure the rights of the individual are protected and that no one else connected with the behavior change project experiences any adverse side effects. We refer to this code of ethics as *responsible conduct*.

Behavior analysts have created a new level of professional recognition. The Board Certified Behavior Analyst (BCBA) certification is rapidly becoming accepted around the world as the method of determining who is qualified to practice in this field. There are two levels of certification: (a) BCBA (for those who have a minimum of a bachelor's and a master's degree), and (b) the Board Certified Associate Behavior Analyst (BCABA; for those who have entry-level training with a bachelor's degree). For the BCBA, 225 classroom hours of instruction must be provided in specific areas, including ethical considerations, principles and processes, behavioral assessment, experimental evaluation of interventions, and measurement. Certification is granted by the national Behavior Analyst Certification Board® (BACB) located in Tallahassee, Florida. The board is overseen by Dr. Jerry Shook who is the executive director. For more information on the board and how to become certified, go to www.bacb.com

As long as they meet the certification requirements, there is some variance in the degrees that behavior analysts may have. The doctor of philosophy (PhD) is a graduate degree that involves research. The PhD has prepared the recipient to become a researcher in addition to being a practitioner.

The doctor of psychology (PsyD) degree, prepares psychologists to be clinical practitioners and interpreters of research. The PsyD degree trains psychologists in assessing, diagnosing, and treating psychological disorders. A PsyD program has an intense emphasis on field work and clinical experience rather than the research that is in a PhD program.

Individuals who wish to have a strong background in education may choose to pursue the doctor of education (EdD) degree. The emphasis in an EdD program is a strong background in education, child development, and learning disabilities, as well as education policy, and clinical/counseling psychology. This degree teaches developmental and educational assessment practices, educational planning, and how to treat of developmental issues.

At the master's degree level, common degrees for behavior analysts include master of arts (MA), master of science (MS), and master of social work (MSW). Whether or not you will get an MA or MS will depend on which degrees are offered at the university you attend. Many MA programs will not require a written thesis, whereas the MS degree usually requires a written research thesis. The MSW is the social work degree with an emphasis on diagnosing and treating psychological problems and providing mental health resources.

● ●

Key Concepts:
Jobs, BCBA

EXERCISES:

1. What are some jobs you can do as a behavior analyst—who can you work with and in what settings?
2. The BACB manages the certification program for behavior analysts. Visit the BACB Web page and describe what you can learn from this page.

QUESTION #38.
What kind of jobs and professional opportunities are available for behavior analysts?

Many exciting, rewarding (and well paying) jobs are available to behavior analysts. In great demand in most states, behavior analysts often work as one-to-one therapists for autistic children who have language deficits and severe behavior problems. There are also many jobs for behavior analysts who wish to work as consultants to educational systems. At a recent Association for Behavior Analysis (ABA) annual meeting in Chicago (May, 2005), there were many jobs posted by employers who were looking for applicants. There were nearly 120 jobs posted, but only 19 behavior analysts had posted cards on the "Looking for a new position" bulletin board.

> **"Many exciting, rewarding (and well paying) jobs are available to behavior analysts."**

Many of the 120 job openings posted at the ABA conference were with consulting firms. Consulting jobs specializing in providing behavioral services to a wide variety of individuals and agencies are available across the country (and in other countries!) for behavior analysts. At ABA, one firm boasted that it had over 100 Board Certified Behavior Analysts on its employee roster and they were looking to expand. Because the demand is outstripping the supply by such a great extent, salaries for behavior analysts are quite good at this time. In 2005, new graduates of master's programs were routinely making over $40,000 for their first position, and some were making as much as $70,000 right out of school.

One of the most useful resources for behavior analysts who are looking for work is the Service to Apply, Recruit, and Train (START) resource on the ABA Web page (http://apps.abainternational.org/start/index.asp). START's mission is to place behavior analysts in jobs, graduate programs, and internships to support the growth of behavior analysis through research, education, and practice. It's on the START Web page that you can post applications for jobs, find employers who are looking to hire behavior analysts, and find a list of graduate programs and available faculty positions.

• •

Key Concepts:
Jobs, professional opportunities, salaries

EXERCISES:

1. Go to a search engine such as www.google.com. In the search box, type "jobs for behavior analysts"—what are some of the jobs that are listed?
2. How do the salaries compare with other entry-level professional jobs?
3. Go to the START section of the ABA Web page (http://apps.abainternational.org/start/index.asp) What kind of job information can you find here? If you were looking for a job today, what jobs would be available?

QUESTION #39.
How do you get started in this field?

The proper foundation for becoming a Board Certified Behavior Analyst is to take an undergraduate course in learning. This course should have an emphasis on operant conditioning and should have a hands-on laboratory, often referred to as a "rat lab." You will learn the basics of behavior principles as they apply to animals as well as the fundamentals of the science of behavior, including shaping, chaining, fading, extinction, and schedules of reinforcement. In addition, you'll learn the distinction between operant and respondent conditioning, discover the basis of conditioned emotional behavior, and learn how this relates to the autonomic responses that underlay fear and anxiety.

After completing a basic learning course, your next step is to take an introductory course in applied behavior analysis. This course will show you how the science of behavior can be applied in a variety of settings from the classroom to the boardroom, from infants to geriatrics, and from the front yard to the football field. After completing the basic ABA course, your next step is to take an individual study course. Some universities call such courses (where you work one on one with a faculty member on a topic that interests you) direct individual study (DIS). A DIS will provide you with an opportunity to get some hands-on experience as a therapist or research assistant. If you can find someone to supervise you, this would be a good time to explore the possibility of accruing "supervised hours of experience" under a qualified Certified Behavior Analyst. If you can meet all of the requirements specified by the Behavior Analyst Certification Board for an Associate certificate (see www.bacb.com for details), you'll be able to sit for the exam, which has been specially designed for students with a bachelor's degree. Some universities now have specialized undergraduate tracks just for this purpose (again, please see www.bacb.com for details). Depending on where you look, there may be a job waiting for you with your bachelor's degree and Associate certificate. This is actually one of the very few ways you can reasonably expect to get a job with a bachelor's degree in psychology. And it could be an exciting way to start a career in behavior analysis. You can work with children or adults who definitely need your expertise and you will learn from being supervised by a BCBA. In addition, you'll be making very good money and this experience will be extremely valuable if you want to go on to graduate school, earn a master's degree, and make behavior analysis your career.

• •

Key Concepts:
Getting started as a behavior analyst

EXERCISES:

1. What kind of university training should you have if you want to be a behavior analyst?
2. In addition to taking college classes, what else can you do to prepare for a job as a behavior analyst?

QUESTION #40.
How do I become a Board Certified Behavior Analyst (BCBA)?

To become a BCBA or a Board Certified *Associate* Behavior Analyst, you will need to complete a special set of behaviorally oriented courses taught by qualified CBA faculty, engage in several hundred hours of supervised experience under a BCBA, and then take and pass a rigorous exam on the basic concepts of behavior analysis and their application.

Once you are certified, you are eligible for job openings anywhere in the world where "Certified Behavior Analyst" is recognized as a credential. You can be certified at either the bachelor's or master's level, and once you receive your certification, you are required to complete a certain number of continuing education hours each year (this varies for the CBA and CABA). For further information, go to: www.bacb.com, the Web page of the Behavior Analysis Certification Board®.

• •

Key Concepts:
Getting certified, BCBA

EXERCISES:

1. How do you become certified as a behavior analyst?
2. Go to the Behavior Analyst Certification Board Web page and look at the applications for certification as a behavior analyst and as an associate behavior analyst. What are the differences?

QUESTION #41.

Can I receive certification while I am in graduate school?

The answer to this question is fairly short: yes. Most of the 75 or so programs that are preapproved by the Behavior Analyst Certification Board prepare you to take the Certified Behavior Analyst exam right at the end of your last semester or shortly after you graduate. If you don't have your Associate certificate when you start your master's program, you should be able to complete all the requirements for this during your first year of graduate school and then sit for the exam at the end of the first year. You will need to talk with the person in charge of the graduate program for details on this.

· ·

Key Concepts:
Graduate school, getting certified, Certified Behavior Analyst exam, Board Certified Behavior Analyst

EXERCISE:

1. How soon can you take the exam for certification as a behavior analyst?

QUESTION #42.
What is the daily routine of a behavior analyst?

There are as many daily routines as there are behavior analysts. The daily routine very much depends on the population involved, as well as the location where the behavior analyst is working. If you are working as an associate in a school system, there is a very good chance that you will be assigned to certain teachers who are having a lot of behavior problems in their classrooms. Over the course of the year you might work in two or three different schools, depending on the specific needs of the school system.

On the other hand, if you have been trained to work with autistic children and have experience doing one-on-one therapy in language acquisition and social skills training, you will probably be working in the children's homes 2 to 4 hours a day. In this case, you might work with only one child or perhaps two children for your whole caseload. Other autism therapists are hired by the school system and may work with a small class of autistic children under the supervision of a lead teacher, who is probably a certified behavior analyst.

Some behavior analysis jobs provide opportunities for travel. A recent ad announcing a job for a behavior analyst read: "Wanted: full time behavior analyst to work with our autistic child in our home in Aspen. Must be willing to travel with the family to Greece during the summer months. Room and board plus salary." This exceptional position paid $50,000 per year.

If you are a behavior analyst who has a master's degree or PhD and are trained in performance management, you will probably be working for a business-consulting firm. Here you will be assigned to work with large companies to help them increase their employees' performance, improve their safety records, enhance sales, reduce waste or paperwork, or solve any number of other interesting human performance problems that occur in large businesses. Consulting contracts for such large companies often extend over a 6-month period or more and you might be working with two such companies each week. One performance management consultant described his workweek like this:

> On Monday morning I fly to Houston and consult with NASA engineers for two days, then I fly to Milwaukee and do executive coaching with the vice president of the fourth largest insurance company in the United States. On Thursday night I fly back to Atlanta and spend Friday in the office meeting with my supervisor and other colleagues and filing reports on my week's work. On Monday morning I'm headed back to Houston. The desk clerks at the Marriott know me by my first name and when I walk in the door to check in, they say, 'Welcome home.'

His salary is near six figures.

Finally, if you ever have the occasion to attend the annual conference of the Association for Behavior Analysis (ABA), you'll be able to learn about the many academic positions for behavior analysts. At the PhD level there are teaching and research positions in a number of universities, colleges, and community colleges in the United States and in several other countries. ABA is a place you can go to market your skills and find the perfect match between you and a prospective employer.

The skills of a behavior analyst would be beneficial in almost every type of work setting. If you are a behavior analyst and you have a strong desire to work in a setting that does not have a behavioral position, one solution is to accept a job for which you are qualified and that you can do well. Within the context of the job that already exists, you can use your behavioral skills to make a difference and before long, you'll be indispensable.

• •

Key Concepts:
Daily routine for a behavior analyst

EXERCISE:

1. Talk to someone who is a behavior analyst. Ask the behavior analyst to describe his or her job in terms of the daily routine.

QUESTION #43.
Do you always work one on one with clients?

The one specialization where you work one on-one with clients is in the area of autism. This is because the research has shown that this form of behaviorally based training is more likely to produce positive results than any other form of treatment for autistic children. Ivar Lovaas published the seminal article demonstrating the power of the so-called discrete-trial method that is used by many behavior analysts and therapists (Lovaas, 1987). This method was described in detail in Catherine Maurice's (1993) now-classic book, and it single-handedly ignited a demand for behavior analysts to work with this most difficult population. Lovaas's research showed that autistic children diagnosed early enough so that they could get intensive one-on-one discrete-trial training for up to 8 hours per day could actually "recover" from autism; that is, when they were placed in kindergarten classes after at least 2 years of therapy they were indistinguishable from "normal" children. Catherine Maurice's two autistic children had this exact result. In her wonderful book, *Let Me Hear Your Voice* (Maurice, 1993), she extolled the virtues of operant-based training and the combination of researcher–parent cooperation. This was all that was needed to motivate parents all over the country to seek behavior analysts to help their children with autism. Since the Lovaas article was published, numerous methods have evolved that blend discrete-trial training with other approaches. These combinations of approaches depart in some respects from his initial model. Children with less severe autism, for example, might benefit from some small group instruction or from imbedded (i.e., discrete-trial training inserted into the normal curriculum) classroom instruction.

A fundamental tenet of behavior analysis is that behavior is a function of the environment (plus whatever history of reinforcement the person has acquired). Thus, most behavior problems that are referred to us are maintained by something in the existing environment of the individual, something that needs to be changed to produce a change in the person's behavior.

Bartenders who are supposed to clean up the bar and close it for the night but who often fail to do this probably don't need therapy or training. What they probably need is regular feedback from their environment, which includes the owner of the bar and the manager on duty. A behavior analyst consulting with a bar owner can set up a data collection and feedback system that will be enforced by the owner through the manager to determine employee reinforcers and contingencies to be put in place. In a case like this, the behavior analyst might never even interact with the bartenders who are the subject of the study. Likewise, behavior analysts who are working as consultants in a sheltered workshop may devise contingencies of reinforcement to encourage these clients with developmental disabilities to stay on task, engage in safe behaviors, and increase their productivity, without necessarily engaging them one on one. In this case the one-on-one time will be spent with the workshop managers and supervisors.

● ●

Key Concepts:
One-on-one training, discrete-trial training, Ivar Lovaas

EXERCISES:

1. Do behavior analysts always work one on one with clients? What settings/skills require that clients receive one-on-one training?
2. Of his many contributions, what is one contribution Ivar Lovaas has made to teaching children with autism?

QUESTION #44.

What skills are involved in being successful in applied behavior analysis?

To be a successful behavior analyst, you do not need to be a whiz at statistics, but there are many other skills that are essential. First of all, you need to be a "people person," that is someone who enjoys being around others, noting informally what they do, looking for relevant consequences, and analyzing their behavior. Because your stock in trade is behavior, and behavior is all around, you should be a curious person, someone who is observant, who feels comfortable asking questions, and who can remain nonjudgmental about the answers.

Behavior analysts are first and foremost problem solvers, so you have to be comfortable in this role; you have to be able to think outside the box, as the expression goes, because you will almost constantly be troubleshooting some aspect of behavior programming and looking for new, creative solutions. To be a good behavior analyst, you have to be very good at explaining things to people, sometimes to total strangers. Effective behavior analysts are very good at thinking on their feet about how to define a problem behavior and how to measure it accurately and reliably. You also must be prepared to put your ideas for behavior change to the test of the data and be willing to change your position if your solutions don't pan out.

One trait that very successful behavior analysts have is that they are able to establish themselves quickly as reinforcers. *Friendly, trustworthy,* and *charismatic* are words often used to describe successful people, and these terms apply to good behavior analysts as well. You need to be very comfortable in giving people positive feedback, praising their work, noticing little things that they do are perfect or darn near perfect, and being able to describe the behaviors objectively and sincerely.

Sometimes, as a behavior analyst, you might be the one getting the feedback. You might have to interact with others who do not value the behavioral approach. While remaining professional and friendly, along with cool, calm, and collected, there will be times that you will be the underdog and will need to be a little "thick skinned."

Other skill sets that are essential are an ability to write quickly and effortlessly, to manage your time wisely with little supervision, and meet daily and weekly deadlines for reports, behavior programs, and related memos. Behavior analysts are often the chairs of treatment committees, so you will need to feel comfortable running a meeting, delegating work to others, and asking them to present their results to your committee. Again, all of this must be done in a very friendly fashion, with you showing no signs of stress or fear of failure.

Finally, behavior analysts must be able to think analytically, that is, they must be able to think in terms of a logical series of steps and options confronted each day. Behavior analysts set priorities for things that need to be done, check them off, and then proceed to the next step with out being sidetracked. You will need to constantly evaluate your own performance (many behavior analysts take data on their own behavior, setting goals, rewarding themselves when they meet a particularly challenging objective, and then shaping themselves for higher goals).

This may seem like a tall order, but it is clear that anyone going into this profession who has any significant deficits in any of these areas is going to find this a very frustrating business indeed. The rewards of being a behavior analyst are great; this has to be one of the most satisfying jobs in the world today. As a behavior analyst, you can set children on the road to success with language and social skills, help adolescents turn their lives around, train a supervisor to be more effective with employees, or train a teacher to be more successful with her students. Watching people acquire skills they would never have thought possible—all because you figured out the right task analysis or were able to put new powerful reinforcers in place—has to be one of the most significant achievements that anyone in the helping professions would aspire to accomplish.

Working as a behavior analyst is not for those who love a routine and who must know exactly what will happen each day they go to work. Each new day will bring different, unconventional challenges to overcome, new people to persuade to try a different approach, frustrations over a behavior program that didn't work, and the excitement of taking on a new case. The work is never boring and is quite unpredictable. It keeps you on your toes and keeps your mind busy thinking up new ways to train, to modify contingencies, and to apply what you know about human behavior.

● ●

Key Concepts:
Success as a behavior analyst, characteristics of jobs

EXERCISES:

1. Make a checklist of the aptitudes and skills needed to be a good behavior analyst.
2. Using your checklist, check off the items you feel that you have. Are there any areas you need to work on?

QUESTION #45.
What steps do you need to take to work competitively in this field?

Assuming that you want to go on to a graduate program and earn at least a master's degree with a specialization in applied behavior analysis, you will want to set your sights on getting into the best program you can. This means having a terrific GPA (3.5 or higher), very strong GRE scores (1200 total is an excellent score; 1000 is the minimum for most graduate programs) and three strong letters of recommendation from faculty that you've worked with as an undergraduate.

You should start investigating graduate programs the summer before you graduate (assuming you are graduating at the end of spring semester). A good place to start is with your faculty advisor or the faculty member who teaches the applied behavior analysis courses. You should also go to the Association for Behavior Analysis (ABA) Web site and check out their Graduate Training Directory (at www.abainternational.org/start/findgtd.asp). Look for a graduate program with the specialty you are interested in and determine what their requirements are. Assuming you meet the qualifications, you may want to contact one of the faculty members with whom you'd like to work, ask a few questions about the program, and, if possible, arrange a visit. We can't stress enough the importance of this step. If you are very interested in working with infants as a career, you won't want to end up by default with a major professor whose primary interest is behavior analysis in business settings. If you are from Florida and you want to specialize in an area where the country's foremost expert is in Michigan, do whatever it takes to be trained by that person. Far too often, students make a decision that impacts their lives forever when they decide that they don't want to be inconvenienced by cold weather, they will die if they can't move to where a boyfriend is living, or they want to be near their parents and friends during graduate school. Don't let geography prevent you from being all you can be.

In graduate school, you'll want to put forward your very best effort because this will be your chance to impress faculty members with your keen intelligence, your tireless work ethic, your undying spirit—you can fill in the rest, you know the speech by heart. It is probably a good idea to develop some considerable expertise in one or two areas of behavior analysis. If you want to work as an autism therapist you will definitely want to get plenty of experience with a wide variety of behavioral problems in this field. For example, in addition to taking advantage of every opportunity to work with autistic or language-delayed children, you could go to local workshops on the topic, perhaps do a summer internship with some organization that works with children with autism, or you could perform some volunteer hours with a local organization that serves children with disabilities. For whatever specialty you are interested in, there will be a way for you to put in extra time and gain additional experience beyond what is offered in the classroom. Reading everything you can get your hands on about your area of interest is a good idea. Talk to faculty who do research and volunteer to help. If you have no interest in research or the idea of reading to learn more about an area doesn't appeal to you, you may want to rethink your plan to attend graduate school.

Work hard, work smart, volunteer, get involved, and you'll get ahead in graduate school. While you are in graduate school, go to as many state and national conferences as you can and meet as many people as you can. Build your network, because it is this network that will provide leads for good jobs once you are on the market. If you have impressed your faculty, they should be eager to recommend you for the very best jobs that are coming open. If you've done your networking, you should have a long list of people you can call when the time is right to make your announcement, "Hi, remember me from the California ABA conference? Well, I'm graduating in August and I heard you had an opening. I'd like to send you my resume, if that's okay. You'll notice on there that I'm giving a talk at ABA."

Key Concepts:

Getting into graduate school, grades

EXERCISE:

1. To become certified as a behavior analyst, you'll need to go to graduate school. Check the ABA Web site and select three master's programs near you. What are the minimum entry requirements for these programs?

QUESTION #46.

How does the applied behavior analysis relate to performance management?
I think I might be interested in working in a business setting when I graduate.

Performance management is the application of basic principles of behavior in business, industry, and organizations to improve behaviors that lead to measurable performance outcomes (Daniels & Daniels, 2004). Performance management is a subset of the larger field of applied behavior analysis. The basic concepts and principles are the same, but when they are applied in business and industry there are some special considerations that have to do with the nature of human behavior in the workplace that have to be taken into account. Just as there is a requirement in ABA to conduct a functional analysis prior to putting an intervention in place, there is a movement to insist that performance management business consultants try to determine the cause of performance problems in the business site. This may involve doing an ABC Analysis (in which the relationship of *antecedents*, *behavior*, and *consequences* are analyzed). Either of these strategies will assist the performance management consultant to find the likely controlling variables for the poor service or unprofitable sales performance. In business and industry, because we are not dealing with abnormal or maladaptive behaviors, it is essential that the consultant look for variables such as a lack of goals—or perhaps just poorly stated goals—for employees; inadequate training is also a prime suspect in analyzing deficient performance. Motivation is almost always a problem in business and industry settings where people are paid by the hour or on salary and those who produce very little are paid the same as those who are highly productive. The performance management consultant must be an expert at finding just the right variables to manipulate because there is a great deal on the line in terms of quality customer service, reducing waste, decreasing injuries, and increasing margins (profits).

Key Concepts:
Performance management, business and industry

EXERCISES:

1. Go to the Aubrey Daniels International Web site (www.aubreydaniels.com). What services does this performance management consulting firm offer?
2. Look at PM E-zine, an online performance management magazine (www.pmezine.com). Find some examples of performance management projects.

Nine

Behavior Analyst Code of Ethics

QUESTION #47.

Is there a code of ethics that behavior analysts must follow?

Musicians Crosby, Stills, and Nash started a hit song with, "You, who are on the road, must have a code, that you can live by." To answer your question, yes, behavior analysts who are board certified have a code that we can live by. *The Guidelines for Responsible Conduct* have been adopted by the Behavior Analyst Certification Board (Bailey & Burch, 2005). These guidelines spell out the rights of clients who are treated by behavior analysts (the right to effective treatment, consent, confidentiality, functional assessment, and so on) and they set very high standards for those who provide treatment. As behavior analysts we have to meet a stringent set of academic standards in our training and must keep current with new developments through continuing education that includes courses and workshops on ethics. Behavior analysts are required to use only methods that have a scientific base and must make program changes based on data collected for each individual client. They must use the least restrictive procedures, avoid harmful reinforcers, and have measurable criteria for terminating a program.

Behavior analysts who are not board certified but who are members of the Association for Behavior Analysis: International must abide by the code of ethics published by the American Psychological Association.

If you are in need of a behavior analyst to work with you or a member of your family, it would be a good idea to inquire as to whether or not the behavior analyst you are considering is board certified and agrees to adhere to *The Guidelines for Responsible Conduct*. The purpose of the guidelines is to assure that only the safest and most effective procedures are used with clients, that they are the least restrictive methods available, and only qualified personnel are involved in treatment.

Key Concepts:

The Guidelines for Responsible Conduct, **code of ethics, ethics**

EXERCISE:

1. Go to the Web site of the Behavior Analyst Certification Board (www.bacb.com). Look at the guidelines that are the code of ethics for our field. List the 10 major areas covered in the guidelines.

QUESTION #48.

Do behavior analysts believe in punishment?

This is a difficult and somewhat touchy subject, but it is a great question that raises lots of issues about how behavior analysts think about certain kinds of problems. First of all, in the culture, there is a lot of confusion about the terms *punishment* and *punish*. People often hear the word *punishment* and think immediately of moral retribution and parents who, in a fit of rage, send small children to bed without their supper. This is absolutely not what behavior analysts are talking about when they use the word *punishment*.

Let's start with a definition of *punishment*. When behavior analysts speak of punishment, they are referring to a scientific term. Generally speaking, we would define a *punisher* as a consequence; this consequence follows a behavior and decreases the probability that the behavior will occur again in the future. This is what we call a *functional definition*. Punishment is defined by its effects; it decreases future behavior. (Punishment can also involve taking away something as well. This is how fines work.) Punishers can be as mild as giving someone a look of disapproval, putting a child in time-out for 1 minute, or saying "No!" to get a toddler to stop a behavior. We need to remember that, just like reinforcers, punishers can be very individualized; what is punishing to one person may not be to another. You might scream at your roommate, partner, or spouse for leaving dirty dishes in the living room. If the behavior stops, your screaming was a punisher. If the roommate continues to leave dirty dishes, your screaming was not a punisher. If punishment is to work effectively, it should be delivered immediately following (or possibly during) the behavior to be reduced. And, it's a bad idea to start with a mild punisher and gradually work up to a more severe one—the person will likely just adapt to the punishment and it will be ineffective.

Although some may argue that punishment should not be used because it doesn't work, the research in operant conditioning and in applied research does not support this conclusion. Punishment does work; the question is whether we should use it or not, that is, are there other alternatives that might be better? One reason we want to consider alternative ways of decreasing behavior is that punishment—although it works—can have very serious side effects. When punishment is delivered by a person, the person can become paired with this aversive event. For example, if a teenager's father beat him with a belt for stealing, the young man could come to hate his father even though he might have recognized stealing was an unacceptable behavior. Punishment can elicit aggression and the teen who is hit with a belt might beat up his little sister shortly after the session with the belt. Punishment also sets the occasion for escape and avoidance responding. Given the earlier scenario, for example, if punishment was frequent and intense, the teen might start by avoiding his dad around the house and ultimately escape altogether by running away. A high percentage of teen who run away each year report that they couldn't stand the punishment they received and were prepared to take their chances on their own in the real world.

There is an extensive literature on the use of punishers in applied behavior analysis. Everything from lemon juice to Tobasco® sauce to electric shock has been used to decrease or eliminate certain behaviors. Again, the major concern here is not that punishment doesn't work, but rather that it is a highly inappropriate way to change behavior. We now have much more effective ways of reducing or eliminating behavior that involve primarily the use of positive reinforcement for competing or

other behaviors. So, to eliminate a little girl's hand biting, for example, we would arrange to reinforce her for playing with toys or brushing her hair. Using reinforcement in this manner sidesteps all the nasty side effects of punishment.

One further reason for not using punishment is in clinical settings, such as treatment facilities for severely handicapped individuals with very dangerous self-injurious behaviors, the punisher always has to be delivered by some staff member. The concern is this person may not be consistent in the use of the punisher. Although a treatment specialist might be well trained in the use of the punisher, he or she might make a mistake and punish the wrong behavior or may try to use it with another resident. Such unauthorized uses of punishers are unethical in the extreme, and for this reason alone behavior analysts would think seriously about recommending the use of punishment for a client.

At an early point in the history of behavior analysis it was not uncommon for punishment to be used to decrease behaviors. We have since learned that the side effects of punishment are so great and the risk of misuse so high that punishment is hardly ever recommended any more. In the behavior analyst code of ethics, it is recommended that if punishment is necessary, it should always be accompanied by a reinforcer for appropriate behavior. When it comes to treatment plans, remember what Johnny Mercer said in his 1944 song: "You gotta accentuate the positive. Eliminate the negative.... Don't mess with mister in-between!"

● ●

Key Concepts:
Punishment, functional definition, side effects, escape and avoidance

EXERCISES:

1. Think back on a time when you were punished for something. Did you repeat the behavior? Did you have any hard feelings toward the person who punished you?
2. Have you had occasion to punish someone for a bad behavior? How did the punishment work? Do you now wish you had thought of another course of action?

QUESTION #49.

Is it ethical to try to change someone else's behavior without his or her permission?

In the professional setting, where we're talking about clients, you must follow *The Guidelines for Responsible Conduct* and obtain all necessary permissions (from the client or client representative) to work on behavioral issues. You must also follow all of the recommendations in the guidelines about procedures, including taking a baseline, evaluating data, and modifying the program as needed.

But we assume this isn't what you're asking about. You're asking about your husband, who throws wet towels in the laundry hamper so all of your clothes get wet and full of mildew before you wash them. Or maybe you're talking about your sister, who calls far too often to complain, complain, and complain about everyone in the family.

So, your question is, if you've got the skills, is it ethical to try to change the behavior of these people? We think it is. You'll be using prompts, a ton of reinforcement for appropriate behavior, some extinction of inappropriate behavior, and in some cases, some "job aids." An example job aid for Mr. Mildew, who needs help with his wet towels, would be a sign near the laundry hamper saying, "No wet towels please—Love, the Management."

Sometimes when we need to change a behavior, it involves changing the behavior of someone who is being insensitive or rude in public. Not too long ago, smoking was allowed everywhere. Out of habit, some smokers would light up on planes and trains, in restaurants and pubs, causing discomfort and physical suffering for anyone in the room with allergies or asthma. Some people suffered in silence; others began a revolution by asking, "Would you mind?" as they waved their hands in front of their faces. Due to new local and state ordinances and laws, cigarettes are no longer a problem—"No Smoking Area" signs are everywhere and nonsmokers can breath easily again.

Sadly, it seems, cell phones are the new cigarettes. You're enjoying a fancy meal in upscale restaurant when you hear that familiar sound and someone at a nearby table takes a call and proceeds to talk noisily about nothing; your quiet, relaxing meal is ruined. One way to handle this is by reverting to your antismoking-campaign days: "Excuse me, would you mind taking that call outside?" In settings where cell phones are an ongoing problem, you can ask the management to post a sign at the entrance or in the lobby to serve as an antecedent stimulus to indicate "Quiet Zone. Please take cell calls outside." Signs for such quiet zones are being posted in an increasing number of restaurants, airport frequent flyer lounges, doctor's offices, gyms, and other settings where people need a break.

The first author recently encountered a "natural" when it comes to the use of behavioral skills to shape interpersonal interactions. In a physical rehabilitation clinic, a physical therapist we'll call Jerrod was observed working with patients suffering from back injuries. He would initially talk to them in a soothing, comforting voice, praising any small attempt on the patient's part to move a stiff and tender limb just a few degrees. Then, with very deliberate and practiced skill, he would raise the bar just a little, "Can you try 10 more bridges for me? Just give it a shot and let's see how you do." Jerrod would smile and then flash a big grin and give the patient a big high five when he or she succeeded. "You did it; that's just great! God bless! Now, let's see if you can do two sets of 10 press-ups. You did one set last time; I think you're ready." Jerrod was a master behavior shaper, using subtle prompts to do more, keeping a straight face and looking intent when there was no improvement, "Maybe next time," he would say in his flat tone. Later on when his patients had progressed a good bit, he would put them on an intermittent schedule of reinforcement, asking them to do four sets of 10 repetitions. "I'll check back with you in just a minute," he'd say. "Let me check on another patient." Jerrod gradually raised the criteria (shaping), carefully thinned out the schedule of reinforcement, and used the power of his friendly demeanor, his big smile, and his enthusiastic, "You did it! Fantastic!" as a routine part of his job. He had no training in behavioral psychology and was totally unaware of what he was doing, except that it worked. The only difference between a behavior analyst practicing the use of behavior shaping and Jerrod using the exact same procedures is a knowledge of the science of behavior.

When you can use behavioral procedures to save relationships with the people you love, you're doing them a huge favor. You might initially get some resistance, "What is this ... Pick-on-Cindy Day?" but if you keep your behavior analyst hat on, don't get emotional, dish out lots of contingent reinforcers, and remain consistent, it won't be long before you and Sis can laugh and enjoy each other on the phone.

● ●

Key Concepts:
Ethics and changing behavior of others

EXERCISE:

1. List some of the behaviors you'd like to change of others around you, including family members, friends, roommates, or people in the service industry. Then, list
   (a) where you've gone wrong in handling these issues before. How are you reinforcing and maintaining these behaviors?
   (b) how you can handle the behavioral concerns using sound, systematic behavioral procedures.

QUESTION #50.

When you are introduced to someone as a behavior analyst, what do you say when a person asks if you are going to analyze his or her behavior?

I f you're a behavior analyst and it hasn't happened to you yet, get ready, because it will happen. You'll be at a party having a jolly good time meeting new people. The food is great and the conversation is lively. Then someone will find out that you're a behavior analyst and he or she will say, "Oh! So, you're a behavior analyst. Are you analyzing my behavior?"

One possible answer is, "Yes, I am, and you are in serious need of help." Another possible answer is, "If you want to pay me my assessment fee, I'll analyze your behavior; otherwise I'm just here to eat and enjoy myself like everyone else." But remember, we're behavior analysts and we are trying to win friends and influence people. You can ignore the question, smile, and say, "Isn't this a great party?" and change the direction of the conversation. Or, you can offer nicely, "Do you know much about

behavior analysis?" If the person says no, you can tell him or her where you work and something about what you do.

Light-hearted jokes with people you know are acceptable, as long as they are in good taste. The main thing to remember is that when you find yourself in a social situation in which someone knows what you do for a living, this is a chance for you to represent the field to other people.

● ●

Key Concepts:
Behavior analysts in social situations

EXERCISE:

1. Groups that teach professionals how to speak in public have exercises designed to teach you to get your message across in a short period of time. One exercise is to assume you are at a Chamber of Commerce meeting; you have 1 minute to stand up, say that you are a behavior analysis consultant, and tell what you do. Use a stopwatch. What would you say?

References and Recommended Reading

Analysis of Verbal Behavior. (Published annually by the Association for Behavior Analysis: International). Available from http://www.abainternational.org/avbjournal/currentissue.asp

Austin, J., Weatherly, N. L., & Gravina, N. E. (2005). Using task clarification, graphic feedback, and verbal feedback to increase closing-task completion in a privately owned restaurant. *Journal of Applied Behavior Analysis, 38,* 117–120.

Baer, D., Wolf, M., & Risley, T. (1968). Some current dimensions of applied behavior analysis. *Journal of Applied Behavior Analysis, 1,* 91–97.

Bailey, J. S., & Burch, M. R. (2002). *Research methods in applied behavior analysis.* Thousand Oaks, CA: Sage.

Bailey, J. S., & Burch, M. R. (2005). *Ethics for behavior analysts.* Mahwah, NJ: Lawrence Erlbaum Associates, Inc.

Behavior Analysis Certification Board®. Available from http://www.bacb.com

Burch, M. R., & Bailey, J. S. (1999). *How dogs learn.* New York: Howell Book House.

Buzan, D. S. (2004, March 12). I was not a lab rat. *The Guardian,* pp. 1–4.

Casey, P., Armstrong, M., Calabrese, D. N., Celenza, M., Cooper, A., Kleinrichert, I., LeVine, A., & Rubin, C. (Directors). (2005, December 22). Mean Girls [Television broadcast]. In C. P. Stewart (Producer), *Dr. Phil.* Culver City, CA: King World Productions.

Dallery, J., & Glenn, I. M. (2005). Effects of an Internet-based voucher reinforcement program for smoking abstinence: A feasibility study. *Journal of Applied Behavior Analysis, 38,* 349–358.

Daniels, A. C., & Daniels, J. E. (2004). *Performance management: Changing behavior that drives organizational effectiveness.* Atlanta, GA: Performance Management Publications.

Encarta® world English dictionary. (1999). Redmond, WA: Microsoft.

Epstein, R. (1997). Skinner as self-manager. *Journal of Applied Behavior Analysis, 30,* 545–568.

Ericsson, K. A., & Simon, H. A. (1993). *Protocol analysis: Verbal reports as data.* Cambridge, MA: Bradford Books/MIT Press.

Foxx, J., & Roland, C. (2005). The self-esteem fallacy. In: J. Jacobson, R. Foxx, & J. A. Mulick (Eds.), *Controversial therapies for developmental disabilities.* Mahwah, NJ: Lawrence Erlbaum Associates, Inc.

Green, G. (1996). Early behavioral intervention for autism: What does research tell us? In C. Maurice, G. Green, & S. Luce, (Eds.), *Behavioral intervention for young children with autism*. Austin, TX: Pro-Ed.

Guthrie, E. R. (1944). Personality in terms of associative learning. In J. McV. Hunt (Ed), *Personality and the behavior disorders*. New York: The Ronald Press.

Higgins, S. T., Budney, A. J., Bickel, W. K., Foerg, F., Donham, R., & Badger, G. J. (1994). Incentives improve outcome in outpatient behavioral treatment of cocaine dependence. *Archives of General Psychiatry, 51,* 568–576.

Iwata, B. A., Dorsey, M. F., Slifer, K. J., Bauman, K. E., & Richman, G. S. (1982). Toward a functional analysis of self-injury. *Analysis and Intervention in Developmental Disabilities, 2,* 3–20.

Jacobson, J., Foxx, R., & Mulick, J. A. (2005). *Controversial therapies for developmental disabilities*. Mahwah, NJ: Lawrence Erlbaum Associates, Inc.

Johnson, B. M., Miltenberger, R. G., Egemo-Helm, K., Jostad, C. M., Flessner, C., & Gatheridge, B. (2005). Evaluation of behavioral skills training for teaching abduction-prevention skills to young children. *Journal of Applied Behavior Analysis, 38,* 67–78.

Journal of Applied Behavior Analysis. Available from http://seab.envmed.rochester.edu/jaba/

Laraway, S., Snycerski, S., Michael, J., & Poling. A. (2003). Motivating operations and terms to describe them: Some further refinements. *Journal of Applied Behavior Analysis, 36,* 407–414.

Lovaas, O. I. (1987). Behavioral treatment and normal educational and intellectual functioning in young autistic children. *Journal of Consulting and Clinical Psychology, 55,* 3–9

Lundervold, D. A., & Lewin, L. M. (1992). *Behavior analysis and therapy in nursing homes*. Springfield, IL: Thomas.

Maurice, C. (1993). *Let me hear your voice: A family's triumph over autism*. New York: Fawcett Columbine.

Michael, J. (1982). Distinguishing between discriminative and motivating functions of stimuli. *Journal of the Experimental Analysis of Behavior, 37,* 149–155.

Michael, J. (1993). *Concepts and principles of behavior analysis*. Kalamazoo, MI: The Association for Behavior Analysis.

Miltenberger, R. G. (2001). *Behavior modification: Principles and procedures*. Belmont, CA: Wadsworth/Thomson Learning.

Miltenberger, R. G., Gatheridge, B. J., Satterlund, M., Egemo-Helm, K. R., Johnson, B. M., Jostad, C., et al. (2005). Teaching safety skills to children to prevent gun play: An evaluation of in situ training. *Journal of Applied Behavior Analysis, 38,* 395–398.

Ninness, C., Rumph, R., McCuller, G., Harrison, C., Ford, A. M., & Ninness, S. K. (2005). A functional analytic approach to computer-interactive mathematics. *Journal of Applied Behavior Analysis, 38,* 1–22.

Palfreman, J. (Director). (1993, October 19). Prisoners of silence. [Television broadcast]. In J. Palfreman (Producer), *Frontline*. Alexandria, VA: Public Broadcast System.

Park, R. (2000). *Voodoo science*. New York: Oxford University Press.

Premack, D. (1965). Reinforcement theory. In D. Levine (Ed.), *Nebraska Symposium on Motivation* (pp. 123–180). Lincoln: University of Nebraska Press.

Roane, H. S., Call, N. A., & Falcomata, T. S. (2005). A preliminary analysis of adaptive responding under open and closed economies. *Journal of Applied Behavior Analysis, 38,* 335–348.

Roll, J. M. (2005). Assessing the feasibility of using contingency management to modify cigarette smoking by adolescents. *Journal of Applied Behavior Analysis, 38,* 463–468.

Ryan, C. S., & Hemmes, N. S. (2005). Effects of the contingency for homework submission on homework submission and quiz performance in a college course. *Journal of Applied Behavior Analysis, 38,* 79–88.

Singer, M., & Lalich, J. (1996). *Crazy therapies: What are they? Do they work?* San Francisco: Jossey-Bass.

Skinner, B. F. (1938). *The behavior of organisms.* New York: Appleton-Century.

Skinner, B. F. (1953). *Science and human behavior.* New York: Macmillan

Skinner, B. F. (1957). *Verbal behavior.* New York: Appleton-Century-Crofts.

Skinner, B. F. (1969). *Contingencies of reinforcement: A theoretical analysis.* New York: Appleton-Century-Crofts.

Skinner, B. F. (1987). A thinking aid. *Journal of Applied Behavior Analysis, 20,* 379–380.

Skinner, B. F., & Vaughan, M. E. (1983). *Enjoy old age: A practical guide.* New York: Norton.

Slater, L. (2004). *Opening Skinner's box.* New York: Norton.

Smith, T., Mruzek, D., & Mozingo, D. (2005). Sensory integrative therapy. In J. Jacobson, R. Foxx, & J. A. Mulick (Eds.), *Controversial therapies for developmental disabilities.* Mahwah, NJ: Lawrence Erlbaum Associates, Inc.

Sulzer-Azaroff, B., & Mayer, R. (1991). *Behavior analysis for lasting change.* Stamford, CT: Wadsworth.

Sundberg, M. L., & Partington, J. W. (1998). *Teaching language to children with autism or other developmental disabilities.* Danville, CA: Behavior Analysts, Inc.

Therrien, K., Wilder, D. A., Rodriguez, M., & Wine, B. (2005). Preintervention analysis and improvement of customer greeting in a restaurant. *Journal of Applied Behavior Analysis, 38,* 411–416.

Tharp, R., & Wetzel, R. (1969). *Behavior modification in the natural environment.* New York: Academic.

United Kingdom Parliament House of Commons health report. (2005). London: United Kingdom House of Commons. Available from www.publications.parliament.uk/pa/cm200405/cmselect/cmhealth/42/4202.htm

Van Houten, R., Malenfant, J. E. L., Austin, J., & Lebbon, A. (2005). The effects of a seatbelt-gearshift delay prompt on the seatbelt use of motorists who do not regularly wear seatbelts. *Journal of Applied Behavior Analysis, 38,* 195–204.

Van Houten, R., Malenfant, J. E. L., Zhao, N., Ko, B., & Van Houten, J. (2005). Evaluation of two methods of prompting drivers to use specific exits on conflicts between vehicles at the critical exit. *Journal of Applied Behavior Analysis, 38,* 289–302.

Wahler, R. G., (1969). Oppositional children: A quest for parental reinforcement control. *Journal of Applied Behavior Analysis, 2,* 159–170.

Wahler, R. G., Vigilante, V. A., & Strand, P. S. (2004). Behavioral contrast in a child's generalized oppositional behavior across home and school settings: Mother and teacher as one? *Journal of Applied Behavior Analysis, 37,* 43–51.

Watson, J. B. (1920). Is thinking merely the action of language mechanisms? *British Journal of Psychology, 11,* 87–104.

Wolf, M., Risley, T., & Mees, H. (1964). Application of operant conditioning procedures to the behaviour problems of an autistic child. *Behavior Research and Therapy, 1,* 305–312.

Zimbardo, P., Johnson, R., & Weber, A. (2006). *Psychology core concepts.* New York: Allyn & Bacon.

Glossary of Terms

Air crib: A specially designed, temperature- and humidity-controlled sleeping environment for infants invented by B.F. Skinner.

Alternative replacement behavior: A behavior that will replace one that is harmful, destructive, or dangerous; chosen to match the function of the original behavior (see also *replacement behavior*).

Analysis: A method of determining the causal variables that produce or maintain a given behavior; often shorthand for functional analysis.

Antecedent: An environmental event or behavior that precedes a specific behavior and sets the occasion for it to occur; may also be referred to as an S^D.

Attention-maintained behavior: A specific behavior that has shown to be a function of attention provided by others.

Autism: A term stemming from the Greek *auto*, meaning "self." A disorder that appears as strikingly abnormal social interactions along with deficit communication and patterns of behavior, usually seen before the age of three.

Behavior: Anything that a person says or does.

Behavioral economics: A subfield of behavior analysis in which responding is viewed as an interaction between price (behavior required) and consumption (reinforcers obtained).

Behavior analysis: An approach to behavior that began with the publication of the *Journal of Applied Behavior Analysis* in 1968 and that emphasizes determining causal variables for socially significant behaviors and developing ethically appropriate treatments that produce socially valid changes for the participants. Also known as *applied behavior analysis*.

Behaviorist: A person who is primarily interested in studying animal and human behavior.

Behavior modification: A term used in the 1960s to describe an approach to behavior that emphasized behavior change using consequences, often aversive consequences. The term is largely out of date and not used by contemporary professionals.

Best practice: A term borrowed from business management to describe the generally accepted best way of doing certain procedures.

Bribery: The offering of money or other incentives to persuade someone to do something, especially something dishonest or illegal.

Certified behavior analyst: A person who has been certified by the Behavior Analyst Certification Board® as qualified to provide behavioral treatment.

Consequences: Environmental changes that occur after a behavior.

Contingencies of reinforcement: A complex interrelationship of behavior and environment that specifies the stimulus, the response, and the reinforcing consequences that generate behavior.

Controlling variables: Those contingencies of reinforcement that have been demonstrated to reliably produce a certain behavior.

Critical thinking: The process of analyzing and evaluating facts and information to determine if the scientific evidence supports a certain proposition.

Data: Quantitative measures resulting from direct observation or other methods with regard to behavior and to independent variables.

Data-based: This is a reference to decisions that are based on objective data, as opposed to opinions, theories, anecdotes, or case studies.

Diagnosis, behavioral: A method of determining the controlling variables for a specific behavior by asking diagnostic questions and testing certain conditions to determine controlling variables.

Diagnostic questions: A series of questions that probe for possible controlling variables.

Differential reinforcement: Following only some selected behaviors with a preselected reinforcer; this is also called *shaping* or *behavior shaping*.

Disease model of behavior: Also known as the medical model; a proposition that certain behaviors result from sickness or disease rather than from contingencies of reinforcement.

Downtrend: An observation of behavioral data that it is trending in a downward direction, usually toward zero occurrences. This is not desirable during baseline, as it can indicate a lack of stability of behavior.

Environment: Objects, people, and events in the immediate surrounding that impinge on sense receptors and that can affect behavior.

Environmental design: The deliberate modification or placement of certain stimuli in the surroundings to produce some behavior change.

Escape and avoidance: An escape response is one that terminates an aversive event; an avoidance response prevents the aversive event from occurring. They often go together as a pair so that a person who learns an escape response often then learns to avoid as well.

Establishing operation: An environmental event that momentarily alters the effectiveness of some other event or consequence. This term has been replaced with the term *motivating operation.*

Evidence-based treatment: This is a movement that began in the 1990s that stressed the need for scientific evidence to support the continued use of treatment. Behavior analysis has been evidence based since its inception in the mid-1960s.

Experimental control: A method of showing with a good deal of certainty that a certain variable was in fact responsible for the behavior change. The reversal or ABAB experimental design does just this by presenting and withdrawing repeatedly some independent variable.

Extinction: A method of reducing a behavior by withholding a previously known reinforcer.

Facilitated communication: A now largely discredited method that purports to help people with speech problems spell out words and sentences. The practice is controversial because a majority of controlled studies have shown that it is not the patient who is producing the words, but the facilitator.

Feedback: A method of providing information on a person's performance. Feedback is generally considered a positive reinforcer.

Functional analysis: An experimental method of determining what the controlling variables are for a given behavior. It involves presenting certain stimuli and consequences, usually in a random fashion over time, and attempting to discover the causes of a behavior in the sense of the maintaining variables for its occurrence and nonoccurrence.

Functional assessment: Generally this includes informal and formal observations including data collection and interviews to determine the likely controlling variables of a behavior. Once a conclusion is reached, the likely "cause" can be tested in a controlled or natural setting to determine if the functional assessment is valid.

Function of behavior: The result or outcome of a behavior.

Generalize, generalization: A behavior trained in one setting may occur in a second setting where no training took place; we would say that the behavior generalized from one setting to another. Or, a behavior is modified through behavioral procedures and then it is observed that a similar behavior now occurs as well; we would say that there has been a generalization of the behavior.

Good Behavior Game: A group contingency used in classroom settings to encourage students to cooperate toward academic goals.

Grandma's Rule: When you eat your vegetables you can have dessert (see also *Premack Principle*).

Group contingency: Used with cohesive groups of individuals, a method of offering reinforcers to each one if the group as a whole meets certain objectives; alternatively a contingency could be set so that if one individual meets certain goals the whole group is reinforced.

History of reinforcement: A theory that the accumulated experiences of contingencies of reinforcement begin to predict future behavior.

Interobserver reliability: A procedure in which two observers independently record behavior and then their data are compared to determine if they are consistent.

Learned behavior: Behavior that is acquired through the learning process rather than reflexive.

Maintaining variables: Those stimuli and consequences that can be shown reliably to produce certain behaviors.

Manipulative behaviors: Behaviors that are maintained by their controlling effects on others, usually thought to be undesirable.

Mediator: A person who serves as the intervention agent in a given situation.

Motivating operation: An environmental event that momentarily alters the effectiveness of some other event or consequence (see also *establishing operation*).

Motivation: A term used to describe the conditions that predictably produce certain behaviors; they generally include the presence of aversive stimuli and certain deprivation conditions such as thirst or hunger.

Noncompliant behavior: The lack of an appropriate response to a specific request.

Obsessive–compulsive disorder (OCD): The repetition of a particular set of behaviors in which the individual appears to be "driven" to repeat a routine or engage in meticulous behaviors such as cleaning the environment or washing the hands. OCD is thought to be an anxiety disorder by psychiatrists but is treatable with cognitive-behavior therapy.

One-on-one treatment: A behavioral method invented by Ivar Lovaas that involves one therapist working for an extended period of time with one client in a behavior-shaping treatment model.

Operant behaviors: Learned behaviors that are controlled by environmental events.

Oppositional defiant disorder: Usually affects children or adolescents who have been shaped by their parents to be disobedient and hostile; this includes extended periods of arguing, loss of temper, anger and resentment toward others, spitefulness, and vindictive behaviors.

Performance improvement plan: In performance management, a proposal to implement a set of procedures to modify behaviors in a business, industry, or organizational setting. The proposal is usually based on an ABC (antecedents, behavior, and consequences) analysis as well as a functional assessment of the pinpointed behaviors.

Performance management: The application of basic principles of behavior in business, industry, and organizational settings to improve human performance.

Placebo effect: The beneficial effect in a patient following a particular treatment that arises from the patient's expectations concerning the treatment rather than from the treatment itself.

Positive reinforcement: A consequence following a behavior that increases the likelihood of similar behavior in the future.

Predictability: The notion that it is possible to determine in advance how a certain individual will behave under specific circumstances.

Premack Principle: Using high-probability behaviors as reinforcers for low-probability behaviors (see also *Grandma's Rule*).

Punishment: A consequence following a behavior that decreases the likelihood of similar behaviors in the future.

Reinforcement: Consequences that follow behavior and increase the likelihood that a behavior will increase in probability.

Reinforcer survey: A method of asking questions of individuals to determine what consequences might serve as reinforcers for the person.

Replacement behavior: Usually a specially selected behavior that is taught to an individual to take the place of a behavior that is dangerous, counterproductive, or bothersome to others.

Respondent behaviors: Behaviors that are elicited by unconditioned stimuli.

Reward: A colloquial term that is used to generally convey the concept of a consequence that is desirable but for which there is no evidence that it changes behavior.

Self-injurious behaviors: Operant behaviors that produce tissue damage to a greater or lesser degree.

Self-management: Procedures used by an individual to change their behavior. These may range from leaving Post-it® Notes to remind oneself to carry out a task to the systematic use of the Premack Principle to manage consequences.

Shaping: A procedure for changing behavior that starts with setting the criterion for reinforcement just a little higher than it was previously.

Single-subject design: A method of using each subject as his/her own control in which through repeated measurements a baseline is established and then various treatment conditions are implemented and then withdrawn.

Socially significant behaviors: Those behaviors that are important to the person because of the consequences that they bring, usually in the form of approval from others; as opposed to trivial behaviors of little consequence.

Social reinforcement: Reinforcers delivered by other persons rather than the natural environment.

Social validation: A set of procedures established by Mont Wolf for determining if the targets of behavior change are supported by the consumer, if the procedures are acceptable, and if the resulting behavior change is acceptable.

Statistically significant effects: Usually effects that are so small that they need to be analyzed or "cooked" by statistical methods to determine if they could have occurred by chance.

Stimulus: A measurable event that may have an effect on behavior.

Talk therapy: A colloquial expression used to describe psychoanalysis, psychotherapy, and counseling, where the major treatment comes from the patient discussing his or her problems with another person.

Theory of behavior: A systematic and comprehensive account of the relationship of behavior to the environment.

Thinking (from a behavioral perspective): According to Skinner (1957), "thinking is behavior" that is covert but nonetheless responds to the same principles as overt behavior. Thinking is learned and can be useful in producing more effective overt behaviors.

Time-out: A method of removing a person from a reinforcing (time-in) environment to one that is less reinforcing; commonly understood to be a punisher for its suppressive effects on behavior.

Token economies: A motivational system in which tokens are given contingent on certain behaviors and then exchanged for reinforcers at a later time for "backup" reinforcers.

Topography: The form of a behavior.

Train for generalization: A method of producing generalization rather than "hoping" for it that involves additional training in those settings where the behavior is desired.

Verbal behavior: Behaviors that are maintained by the behavior of other individuals; specifically, the behavior of a speaker that is maintained by the behavior of a listener.

Appendix

Behavioral Journals

American Journal of Mental Retardation
Analysis of Verbal Behavior
Animal Behavior
Australia & New Zealand Journal of Developmental Disabilities
Behavior Analysis Digest
The Behavior Analyst
Behavior and Social Issues
Behavior Modification
Behavior Therapist
Behavior Therapy
Behavior Research and Therapy
Behavior Therapy and Psychiatry
Behavioral Disorders
Behavioral Interventions
Behavioral Technology Today
Brazilian Journal of Behavior Analysis
Child and Family Behavior Therapy
Education and Treatment of Children
European Journal of Behavior Analysis
Focus on Autism and Other Developmental Disabilities
Journal of Applied Behavior Analysis
Journal of the Association for Severely Handicapped

Journal of Behavior Therapy and Experimental Psychiatry
Journal of Organizational Behavior Management
Journal of Precision Teaching
Journal of School Psychology
Learning & Behavior
Mental Retardation
Mexican Journal of Behavior Analysis
Performance Improvement Journal
Performance Improvement Quarterly
Psychology in the Schools
Research in Developmental Disabilities
School Psychology Review

Author Index

A

Abernathy, W. B., 63
Austin, J., 62

B

Badger, G. J., 107
Baer, D., 10
Bailey, J. S., 48, 75, 128, 151, 175, 180
Bauman, K. E., 8
Bickel, W. K., 107
Budney, A. J., 107
Burch, M. R., 48, 75, 128, 151, 175, 180
Buzan, D. S., 140

C, D

Call, N. A., 62
Dallery, J., 62
Daniels, A. C., 56, 58, 63, 170
Daniels, J. E., 56, 58, 63, 170
Dawson, M., 51
Donham, R., 107
Dorsey, M. F., 8

E

Egemo-Helm, K. R., 62
Epstein, R., 41, 42
Ericsson, K. A., 112, 113

F

Falcomata, T. S., 62
Flessner, C. A., 62
Foerg, F., 107
Ford, A. M., 62
Foxx, J., 115
Foxx, R., 123

G

Gatheridge, B. J., 62
Geller, E. S., 63
Gernsbacher, M. A., 51
Glenn, I. M., 62
Goldsmith, H. H., 51
Gravina, N. E., 62
Green, G., 53
Guthrie, E. R., 24

H, I

Harrison, C., 62
Hemmes, N. S., 62
Higgins, S. T., 107
Iwata, B. A., 8

J

Jacobson, J., 123
Johnson, B. M., 62

Johnson, R., 28
Jostad, C. M., 62

K, L

Khouzam, H. R., 111
Ko, B., 62
Lalich, J., 129
Laraway, S., 114
Lebbon, A., 62
Lewin, L. M., 55
Lovaas, O. I., 52, 162
Lundervold, D. A., 55

M

Malenfant, J. E. L., 62
Maurice, C., xiv, 51, 162
Mayer, R., 37
McCuller, G., 62
Mees, H., 3, 4, 5, 10, 19, 20n
Michael, J., 33, 114
Miltenberger, R. G., 42, 62
Morgan, D. L., 68
Morgan, R. K., 68
Mozingo, D., 129
Mruzek, D., 129
Mulick, J. A., 123

N, P

Ninness, C., 62
Ninsess, S. K., 62
Palfreman, J., 122
Park, R., 129
Partington, J. W., 113
Poling, A., 114
Premack, D., 14

R

Richman, G. S., 8
Risley, T., 3, 4, 5, 10, 19, 20n
Roane, H. S., 62
Rodriguez, M., 62

Roland, C., 115
Roll, J. M., 62
Rumph, R., 62
Ryan, C. S., 62

S

Satterlund, M., 62
Simon, H. A., 113
Singer, M., 129
Skinner, B. F., xxii, 28, 30, 41, 54, 67,
   113
Slater, L., 139
Slifer, K. J., 8
Smith, T., 129
Snycerski, S., 114
Strand, P. S., 29
Sulzer-Azaroff, B., 37
Sundberg, M. L., 113

T, V

Therrien, K., 62
Tharp, R., 20
Van Houten, J., 62
Van Houten, R., 62
Vaughan, M. E., 54
Vigilante, V. A., 29

W

Wahler, R. G., 29, 30
Watson, J. B., 113
Weatherly, N. L., 62
Weber, A., 28
Wetzel, R., 20
Wilder, D. A., 62
Wine, B., 62
Wolf, M., 3, 4, 5, 10, 19, 20n

Z

Zhao, N., 62
Zimbardo, P., 28

Subject Index